中外文**稀有版本**文献

《路德维希·费尔巴哈和德国古典哲学的终结》

英 文 版

【德】弗里德里希·恩格斯 ◎ 著

《路德维希·费尔巴哈和德国古典哲学的终结》的出版与传播

（代序）

马克思主义的产生和发展一直离不开翻译，它同形形色色的错误思潮进行斗争的过程同样离不开翻译。马克思主义奠基人（尤其是恩格斯）极为重视翻译工作，认为这是一项意义重大的革命工作，"马克思的理论正是在目前对社会主义运动产生着巨大的影响"[①]，然而，只有准确翻译出版马克思的著作，才能帮助剔除掉社会主义运动中错误思潮对工人的影响，比如恩格斯打算出版《资本论》的法译本，目的就是希望"使法国人摆脱蒲鲁东用对小资产阶级的理想化把他们引入的谬误观点"[②]。恩格斯同样重视马克思主义著作的翻译，"最近十年国际社会主义文献的巨大增长，特别是马克思和我以前的著作的译本的数量"的增长，认为这些"文献的增加……是国际工人运动本身相应发展的一个象征"[③]。因此，梳理《路德维希·费尔巴哈和德国古典哲学的终结》（简称《费尔巴哈论》）的翻译出版对于了解和掌握社会主义运动的发展和马克思主义的传播情况具有重要意义。

[①]《马克思恩格斯文集》第5卷，北京：人民出版社2009年版，第34页。
[②]《马克思致路德维希·毕希纳（1867年5月1日）》，《马克思恩格斯全集》第31卷，北京：人民出版社1972年版，第546页。
[③]《资本论》第3卷，《马克思恩格斯文集》第7卷，北京：人民出版社2009年版，第3页。

一　《费尔巴哈论》的最初出版和译介

《路德维希·费尔巴哈和德国古典哲学的终结》及其序言是恩格斯晚年时期最重要的著作之一。恩格斯在1886年初接受《新时代》杂志社约稿,以德文写了一篇关于施达克《路德维希·费尔巴哈》的书评。这篇长篇的书评发表在1886年《新时代》杂志第4期和第5期。时隔两年之后,为了便于阅读和传播,恩格斯又于1888年在斯图加特出版单行本,并且给这个单行本写了序言。

这个小册子甫一出版就受到了同情和信仰马克思主义的人(尤其是那些理论家兼革命家)的关注。《费尔巴哈论》出版后不久,法国人就开始关注这个小册子。1894年,巴黎的杂志《新纪元》第4期和第5期上刊登了劳拉·拉法格翻译并经恩格斯审阅过的译文。恩格斯对这个小册子的整个翻译过程都给予了关注。在翻译过程中,恩格斯就给左尔格写信说:"劳拉·拉法格正在把我的《费尔巴哈》译成法文,而且即将在巴黎出版。"① 此外,恩格斯还把这件事情告诉了考茨基,并对这个译本给予了高度评价:"劳拉·拉法格正在把我的《费尔巴哈》译成法文供《新纪元》发表和以后出单行本,狄茨知道这件事定很高兴。前一半我已看过。她的译文忠实而流畅。"②

除了上述译本,《费尔巴哈论》陆续出版了不同语言的译本,它们分别是:(1)1890年,这个小册子的波兰文版翻译出版;(2)1892年,这本书出版了保加利亚文译本;(3)同一年,葡萄牙译本问世。③

---

① 恩格斯:《致弗里德里希·阿道夫·左尔格(1893年12月30日)》,《马克思恩格斯全集》第39卷,北京:人民出版社1974年版,第184页。值得注意的是,我们一般将《路德维希·费尔巴哈和德国古典哲学的终结》简称为《费尔巴哈论》,而恩格斯似乎将之简称为《费尔巴哈》。实际上,我们在后文中还会看到,不同的人对这部著作的简称不尽相同,因此我们在阅读与之相关的文献时要注意这一点。

② 恩格斯:《致卡尔·考茨基(1894年1月9日)》,《马克思恩格斯全集》第39卷,北京:人民出版社1974年版,第190页。

③ 参见《马克思恩格斯文集》第4卷,北京:人民出版社2009年版,第603页,注释168。

然而尽管恩格斯在写《费尔巴哈论》时居住在伦敦，但这本非常重要的小册子的英译本出现得比较晚。根据资料显示，《费尔巴哈论》最早是在1917年翻译成英文的，题目是《费尔巴哈：社会主义哲学的根源》。完整的英译本最早出现在1941年，译者是刘易斯，他还写了评论性导言。截至目前，这个小册子共有四个完整的英文译本，它们分别是1936年杜德编辑出版的收录了马克思和恩格斯关于辩证唯物主义的其他材料的伦敦和纽约版、1941年的纽约版、1946年拉斯克编的莫斯科和伦敦版，以及1950年的莫斯科版（这个版本包括马克思的《关于费尔巴哈的提纲》）。①

尽管处在遥远的东方，日本在马克思主义著作的译介方面并不逊于某些西方国家。《费尔巴哈论》的最早日文本于1927年就已经出现，这在某种程度上不但推动了日本马克思主义的发展，而且还有助于中国马克思主义思想的引介和传播。②

二 《费尔巴哈论》在俄国的传播

作为世界上第一个社会主义国家，单独研究《费尔巴哈论》在俄国的译介出版具有特别的意义。根据已有的文献资料，我们能够判断这

---

① *Feuerbach, The Roots of the Socialist Philosophy*, Translated with a critical introduction by Austin Lewis, Chicago: Charles H. Kerr & Co., 1916.几个完整的译本分别是：(1) *Ludwig Feuerbach and the Outcome of Classical German Philosophy*, With an appendix of other material of Marx and Engels relating to dialectical materialism, Edited by C.P. Dutt, London: Lawrence & Wishart, 1936; New York: International Publishers Co., 1970. (2) *Ludwig Feuerbach and the Outcome of Classical German Philosophy*, New York: International Publishers, 1941. (3) *Ludwig Feuerbach and the Outcome of Classical German Philosophy*, Edited by I.B. Lasker; Moscow: Foreign Languages Publishing House, 1946; London: Lawrence & Wishart, 1947. (4) *Ludwig Feuerbach and the End of Classical German Philosophy*, Moscow: Foreign Languages Publishing House, 1950; Moscow: Progress Publishers, 1969. 这些版本的信息参见尤班克斯编：《马克思恩格斯著作目录和马克思主义参考书目》，北京：书目文献出版社1987年版，第44—45页。

② 关于日文本最早出现年份的判断，本文转引自韩立新：《"日本马克思主义"：一个新的学术范畴》，见〔日〕望月清司：《马克思历史理论的研究》，韩立新译，北京：北京师范大学出版社2009年版，"总序"第3页。关于日本马克思主义对中国马克思主义的影响参见下文第四章第三节的相关内容和注释。

个本子最早受到关注并试图传入的国家之一就是俄罗斯。1889 年,《费尔巴哈论》的俄译文就在圣彼得堡的《北方通报》杂志(第 3 期和第 4 期)上发表了,不过题目改成了"德国古典唯心主义哲学的危机",遗憾的是,在发表的过程中,杂志没有标明作者,仅仅是在文章下面注上了译者格·弗·李沃维奇的署名"格·李·"。关于这个版本与马克思主义之间的关系我们无从考证,但之后几乎所有的译本都与马克思主义组织和马克思主义的传播有关。

(一) 劳动解放社与《费尔巴哈论》翻译出版

我们知道,普列汉诺夫的译本是比较早的,而且也是比较权威的译本。1892 年《劳动解放社》在日内瓦用单行本出版了由格·瓦·普列汉诺夫翻译的全译文。与众不同的是,普列汉诺夫在把弗·恩格斯德文版的《路德维希·费尔巴哈和德国古典哲学的终结》译成俄文后,在出版时附加上了序言和注释,这个序言就是《译者的话》,注释则包括两部分,即:"普列汉诺夫为恩格斯《费尔巴哈与德国古典哲学的终结》一书俄译本第一版所写的注释"和"原校订本第一版的注释"。[①] 他所附加的序言和注释对于我们准确把握马克思主义有着非常重要的作用。但普列汉诺夫的《费尔巴哈论》俄译本之所以能够产生巨大影响,是因为俄国的马克思主义者是在有组织地翻译马克思和恩格斯的著作,而这个组织就是劳动解放社。

劳动解放社,俄国的第一个马克思主义组织,于 1883 年 9 月 25 日在日内瓦成立,于 1903 年解散。这个组织成立伊始就发表了普列汉诺夫起草的被视为劳动解放社成立宣言的文章《关于出版〈现代社会主义丛书〉问题》,其中明确指出俄国"革命的知识分子首先要确立现代社会主义世界观",但当时的社会主义出版物"很难满足"这一要求,

---

[①] 《普列汉诺夫为恩格斯〈费尔巴哈与德国古典哲学的终结〉一书俄译本第一版所写的序言(〈译者的话〉)和注释》,载《普列汉诺夫哲学著作选集》第 1 卷,北京:生活·读书·新知三联书店 1961 年版,第 502—563 页。

因此它开始着手出版《现代社会主义丛书》①,开始"系统地传播马克思和恩格斯的著作"。②

普列汉诺夫认为,《现代社会主义丛书》是一种新的尝试,并提出了自己的主要任务:"(1)通过把马克思和恩格斯学派最重要的著作(注意到不同修养程度的读者需要一些原著)译成俄文的方式,传播科学社会主义思想。(2)从科学社会主义观点和俄国劳动人民的利益出发,批判在我们革命者中间占统治地位的学说,并深入研究俄国社会生活中的最重要的问题。"③ 劳动解放社在组织翻译马克思和恩格斯著作的过程中得到了恩格斯的大力支持和高度评价。恩格斯不但推荐可以优先翻译的著作,替译者解答问题,而且答应对某些著作的翻译给予一切帮助。恩格斯对劳动解放社以及它翻译的自己和马克思的著作最初的俄译本给予了很高评价,认为劳动解放社是"他能够把自己和马克思的著作委托出版的唯一的侨外俄国革命团体"④。

在《现代社会主义丛书》中,劳动解放社选译的重要著作包括《费尔巴哈论》。⑤ 列·阿·列文认为,《现代社会主义丛书》中选译著作的质量比较高,而且这些译本对俄国的社会主义革命运动具有重要意义。此外,这套丛书还有一个优点——"附有译者的序言和注释",但他又认为,"在很多序言和注释中存在严重的错误"。他专门指出,普

---

① 〔俄〕普列汉诺夫:《关于劳动解放社的三篇史料·关于出版〈现代社会主义丛书〉问题》,载《世界历史》1983年第5期,第91页。
② 周邦:《"劳动解放社"的历史地位和作用》,载《国际共运史研究资料》1983年第2期,第30页。
③ 《格·瓦·普列汉诺夫遗著》第8卷第1册,1940年莫斯科版,第29页。另参见《关于出版〈现代社会主义丛书〉问题》以及列文的《马克思恩格斯著作的发表和出版》,周维译,北京:生活·读书·新知三联书店1976年版,第135页。
④ 《格·瓦·普列汉诺夫遗著》第8卷第1册,1940年莫斯科版,第29页。另参见《关于出版〈现代社会主义丛书〉问题》以及列文的《马克思恩格斯著作的发表和出版》,周维译,北京:生活·读书·新知三联书店1976年版,第136页。
⑤ 另外还有4本书,即恩格斯的《社会主义从空想到科学的发展》(1884年、1892年、1902年)、马克思的《关于自由贸易的演说》(1885年)、马克思的《哲学的贫困》(1886年)和恩格斯的《论俄国的社会问题》(1894年)。马克思和恩格斯的这5本著作分别是由普列汉诺夫和查苏利奇翻译完成的,前者翻译的是《关于自由贸易的演说》和《费尔巴哈论》,其余由查苏利奇翻译完成。

列汉诺夫给《费尔巴哈论》写的序言就有观点和立场上的错误，比如他认为普列汉诺夫提到的"象形文字论"就具有"康德主义的符号论"色彩，它是对"马克思主义的认识论"的修正。①

应该说，正是由于劳动解放社，马克思和恩格斯的著作才通过普列汉诺夫等人得到了通俗解释，推动了俄国马克思主义的产生和发展。列宁对此评价道："俄国的马克思主义是在十九世纪八十年代初期的一个侨民团体（劳动解放社）的著作中产生的。"② 这个团体则成了俄国"科学社会主义的奠基者、代表者和最忠实的捍卫者"③，它的理论活动为俄国的社会民主主义运动的发展和工人阶级政党的建立扫清了道路，因而在列宁看来它"在理论上为社会民主主义奠定了基础"，"走了迎接工人运动的第一步"。④

（二）第一次俄国革命时期《费尔巴哈论》的译介和传播

在劳动解放社解散之后，俄国紧接着进入了第一次革命时期（1905—1907 年）。列文认为，这一时期是"在俄国出版和传播马克思和恩格斯著作方面的新的标志"，由于革命形势的发展，政府逐渐放开管制，开始允许在俄国刊印马克思主义的著作。⑤ 在这一时期，马克思主义著作的翻译出版出现了一些新特征，除了像布尔什维克这样的马克思主义者出版马克思和恩格斯的著作，孟什维克也开始关注这一领域。一般来说，在此期间，马克思恩格斯的著作出版在俄国经历了三个阶段："（1）国外阶段，（2）受到审查阶段，（3）不受审查阶段。"⑥

---

① 参见〔苏〕列文：《马克思恩格斯著作的发表和出版》，周维译，北京：生活·读书·新知三联书店 1976 年版，第 133—134 页。
② 《列宁全集》第 15 卷，北京：人民出版社 1959 年版，第 367 页。
③ 周邦："'劳动解放社'的历史地位和作用"，载《国际共运史研究资料》1983 年第 2 期，第 36 页。
④ 《列宁全集》第 20 卷，北京：人民出版社 1958 年版，第 275 页。
⑤ 〔苏〕列文：《马克思恩格斯著作的发表和出版》，周维译，北京：生活·读书·新知三联书店 1976 年版，第 135、154 页。
⑥ 〔苏〕列文：《马克思恩格斯著作的发表和出版》，周维译，北京：生活·读书·新知三联书店 1976 年版，第 160 页。

在第一个阶段（即国外阶段）的 1905 年 7 月，孟什维克编辑出版了一套《科学社会主义丛书》，其中包括恩格斯的《费尔巴哈论》。根据列文的看法，这一版本仍是普列汉诺夫翻译，并新加了长篇序言，扩充了注释，因此是一个相对完整的版本。但是由于普列汉诺夫与孟什维克主义发展的密切关联，所以他的序言和注释中包含着严重的错误，比如，他"把马克思和恩格斯的唯物主义解释成为独特的斯宾诺莎主义"，并对革命中无产阶级的领导权和领袖（即列宁）进行了攻击。然而，随着革命的失败，马克思和恩格斯的个别著作开始被取缔，其中包括恩格斯的《费尔巴哈论》。因而，被保留下来的主要是 1905 年以前的版本。①

（三）苏维埃建立后《费尔巴哈论》的翻译出版

随着十月革命的胜利和苏维埃制度的建立，在苏联党和国家领导人的关心下②，马克思和恩格斯著作的研究、译介和出版传播进入了一个新阶段，苏联不但建立了世界上第一个马克思恩格斯列宁学院，而且对其著作的出版更具规模。当时，国家给马克思恩格斯列宁学院及其杰出的领导人、著名马克思主义文献学家梁赞诺夫规定的任务是"收集、保存、研究和科学地发表马克思、恩格斯……的遗著"③。

为此，马恩学院建立了一个科学图书馆，并于 1923—1926 年间开始拍摄保存在德国社会民主党档案中保存的马克思恩格斯手稿和书信的原件。在广泛收集资料的基础上，马恩（列）研究院在 1928 年开始出版《马克思恩格斯全集》（俄文版第一版）以及《马克思恩格斯文库》

---

① 〔苏〕列文：《马克思恩格斯著作的发表和出版》，周维译，北京：生活·读书·新知三联书店 1976 年版，第 167、161 页。

② 比如，列宁早在 1921 年就询问梁赞诺夫关于马克思恩格斯的书信和著作的收集情况："你们图书馆里有没有从**各种报纸**和某些杂志上**搜集来的**马克思和恩格斯的**全部书信**？……有没有**全部书信的目录**？"2 月 2 日，列宁再次给梁赞诺夫写信："……（5）我们有没有希望在莫斯科收集到马克思和恩格斯发表过的**全部材料**？（6）**在这里已经收集到的材料有没有目录**？(7) 马克思和恩格斯的书信（或复印件）由我们来收集，此议是否可行？"参见《列宁全集》第 50 卷，北京：人民出版社 1988 年版，第 107 页。

③ 〔苏〕列文：《马克思恩格斯著作的发表和出版》，周维译，北京：生活·读书·新知三联书店 1976 年版，第 172 页。

（并不是 MEGA¹），后者主要收录的是马克思恩格斯之前没有发表过的原始文献。① 在苏联，马克思恩格斯著作的出版随着社会形势的变化不断变化，但苏维埃俄国始终重视马克思恩格斯等著作的出版。1933 年，苏联又出版了两卷本的《马克思恩格斯文选》，其主要收录的是"主要的（篇幅不大的）著作"，《费尔巴哈论》被收录于第一卷。

1948 年，国家政治书籍出版社出版了《费尔巴哈论》，其中收录了马克思的《关于费尔巴哈的提纲》。列文认为，这是一个最准确的版本，因为普列汉诺夫之前的译本已经根据德文原文进行了校订和修改。②

《费尔巴哈论》在《马克思恩格斯全集》俄文版的第一版和第二版中均被收录。在俄文版第一版中，它被收录于第 14 卷第 633—678 页，在第二版中被收录于第 21 卷第 267—317、370—371 页。

三 《费尔巴哈论》在国内的译介和传播

在 19 世纪末 20 世纪初，中国面临亡国灭种的大危机，如何走出这种危机，实现民族复兴，几乎成了近现代志士仁人的共同目标。经过数十年的探索，他们认识到只有开启民智、启蒙民众，才能实现救国之目标。毫无疑问，翻译介绍西方思潮是实现启蒙和救亡双重目的的重要途径。梁启超先生在《论译书》中写道："苟其处今日之天下，则必以译书为强国第一义，昭昭然也！"③ 实际上，在中国翻译史上占据重要地位、对中国翻译确定了标准的严复早就认识到了这一点，他指出："然终谓民智不开，则守旧维新两无一可。即使朝廷今日不行一事，抑所为皆非，但令在野之人后生英俊洞识中西实情者日多一日则炎黄种类未必

---

① 〔苏〕列文：《马克思恩格斯著作的发表和出版》，周维译，北京：生活·读书·新知三联书店 1976 年版，第 174—175 页。
② 〔苏〕列文：《马克思恩格斯著作的发表和出版》，周维译，北京：生活·读书·新知三联书店 1976 年版，第 201 页。
③ 梁启超：《论译书》，见《翻译研究论文集（1894—1948 年）》，北京：外语教学与研究出版社 1999 年版，第 10 页。

《路德维希·费尔巴哈和德国古典哲学的终结》的出版与传播（代序）

遂至沦胥；即不幸暂被羁縻，亦将有复苏之一日也。所以屏弃万缘，惟以译书自课。"① 在整个西学东渐的思想大潮和救亡图存的过程中，由于马克思主义的科学性以及在实践上取得的胜利，马克思主义经典著作的翻译同样受到了重视。而在马克思主义所有的经典著作中，恩格斯的《费尔巴哈论》成了最受关注且译本最多的著作之一。

（一）新中国成立前《费尔巴哈论》的中文版本

尽管在新中国成立前还没有国家作为后盾来支持马克思和恩格斯著作的翻译，但他们的著作仍然有不少人感兴趣，而且在某种程度上还不自觉地形成了一种"百花齐放"的局面。恩格斯的《费尔巴哈论》就有多个译本。兹根据出版时间列举如下：

最早的应该是彭嘉生先生的译本，上海南强书局于1929年初出版，书名为《费尔巴哈论》。② 这是一个非常完整的译本，附有恩格斯序言，而且译者在翻译过程中给四章分别加上了小标题："从黑格尔到费尔巴哈""观念论与唯物论""费尔巴哈的宗教哲学及伦理学"和"辩证法的唯物论"。此外，这个译本还有两点值得注意。一是它在附录中增加了五篇文献：（1）马克思的《费尔巴哈论纲》③，（2）恩格斯的《费尔巴哈论》补遗④，（3）恩格斯的《史的唯物论》⑤，（4）马克思的《法兰西唯物史论》⑥，（5）恩格斯的《马克思的唯物论及辩证法》⑦。二是它在正文前附上了董克尔撰写的《编者序言》（写于1927年2月），在

---

① 严复：《严复集》第三册，北京：中华书局1986年版，第525页。
② 有的研究文献认为，《费尔巴哈论》最早的中译本是林超真的译本（该译本的详细情况见下文），但根据笔者的考察，这里似乎存在一些误解。真正的译本应该是彭嘉生的译本。
③ 即马克思版本的《关于费尔巴哈的提纲》。——编者注
④ 编者未能考察出这部分的准确出处。
⑤ 根据译者的注释，这部分取自《社会主义从空想到科学的发展》（译者名之为《从空想到科学的社会主义底发展》）英译本1892年的序言。参见恩格斯：《费尔巴哈论》，彭嘉生译，上海：上海南强书局1929年版，第146页。
⑥ 即《神圣家族》中的"对法国唯物主义的批判的战斗"部分。
⑦ 根据译者的注释，这部分是从马克思的《经济学批判》的评论（1895年）中抄录出来的，但译者又指出恩格斯将这一评论发表于1859年《大众》（Das Volk）上。显然，这个解释存在着矛盾，因此，我们也未能完全判断出这一部分的准确出处，以后有待继续考证之。

书后附有译者后记（写于1929年12月）。这个译本是根据法国人赫尔曼·董克尔（Hermann Duncker）编辑的德文本翻译的，同时参照了英译本和日译本。① 这个译本分别在1932年和1935年进行了再版。中共中央马克思恩格斯列宁斯大林著作编译局（以下简称为"中央编译局"）图书馆收藏了该译本。②

同年12月出版了林超真的译本，其书名接近原书，为《费儿巴赫与德国古典哲学的末日》，而且附有恩格斯的序言、普列汉诺夫的序言（俄文本第二版序）以及《关于费尔巴哈的提纲》。③ 这个译本载于《宗教·哲学·社会主义》。这个译本是根据拉法格等人翻译的法译本翻译过来的④，而且译者在翻译时没有参考恩格斯的德文原文，只有部分内容与俄文进行了对照。

第三个译本是向省吾翻译，书名为《费尔巴哈与古典哲学的终末》。这个译本是全译文，但没有收录序言，该译本由上海江南书局于1930年4月出版。这个版本在目录中标上了五篇附录性文献，但在正文中却没有刊印出来。这个译本与彭嘉生的译本一样，附上了两个序言，即译者序（写于1929年9月）和编者序（亦即赫尔曼·唐克尔⑤所写序言）。这个译本依据的蓝本是德文《马克思主义文库》第3卷，同时参照了日译本。

---

① 为了让读者更加全面地了解早期译者的序言，我们在本书的附录"研究文献精选"中把董克尔的编者序言收录其中。客观讲，尽管这个编者序言与目前的研究比起来比较简略，但它也表明了早期人们对《费尔巴哈论》的关注（角度）。

② 参见《费尔巴哈论》，上海：上海南强书局1929年版。同时参见北京图书馆马列著作研究室编：《马克思恩格斯著作中译文综录》，北京：书目文献出版社1983年版。

③ 名为《马克思：费儿巴赫论纲要》，参见恩格斯：《宗教·哲学·社会主义》，林超真译，上海：亚东图书馆1929年版，第229—372页。

④ Fr. Engels, *Religion, Philosophie, Socialisme*, Traduit Par Paul et Laura Lafargue, Paris, Librairie G. Jacques et Oie, 1901.

⑤ 原文如此，即为董克尔，不同版本译法不同，保留原文译法。——编者注

第四个译本是杨东莼[①]、宁敦伍翻译出版的《机械论的唯物批判论》，它是由上海昆仑书店于1932年5月出版，其中收录了除了马克思恩格斯之外的马克思主义者普列汉诺夫所写的注释。这本书在书后所附的附录最为全备，包括8篇文章：（1）马克思的《费尔巴哈论纲》，（2）恩格斯的《费尔巴哈论》补遗，（3）恩格斯的《史的唯物论》，（4）马克思的《法兰西唯物史论》，（5）恩格斯的《马克思的唯物论及辩证法》，（6）马克思的《费尔巴哈论纲原稿译文》，（7）马克思的《观念论的见解与唯物论的见解之对立》[②]，（8）《蒲列汉诺夫对费尔巴哈的序文和评注》。[③] 书前有《发行者序言》，署名：赫尔曼·唐克尔。

第五个译本是青骊所译，由上海社会主义研究社于1932年11月出版，书名为《费尔巴哈论》。这个译本的最大特点是英汉对照，其中第31—97页为中译文，分四节，每节有标题，文前有序言。这本书的附录也收了马克思的《费尔巴哈论纲》，书前还有中译者序言（写于1932年11月20日）、英译者导言以及《社会主义名著译丛总序》。本书是根据黎威奥斯丁的英文本转译的。

第六个译本是摘译本，译者柳若水以黑格尔哲学批判为主题选取了费尔巴哈、马克思和恩格斯等人的十篇关于黑格尔哲学的著作，撷取其中的重要段落，翻译之后集结成册，书名为《黑格尔哲学批判》。这本书收录的是恩格斯的《费尔巴哈论》的第1节，并将之命名为《从黑

---

① 杨东莼所翻译的最为人所熟知的著作是摩尔根的《古代社会》。摩尔根的书受到了马克思和恩格斯的高度关注，并被二人在不同的文献中大量引用。尽管人们没有研究《费尔巴哈论》与摩尔根的《古代社会》之间的关系，但众所周知，马克思和恩格斯对《古代社会》所做的研究成果都是在《费尔巴哈论》之前出版的，这两本书之间的关系，尽管在文本上没有直接相关性，但在思想上应该是一致的。

② 这部分内容出自《德意志意识形态》（原文译为《德意志观念形态论》）中的"费尔巴哈"章的"一般意识形态，特别是德国哲学"部分。

③ 普列汉诺夫所写的《费尔巴哈论》俄译本第一版序言和第二版序言都收录其中，但与第一版序言密切相关的注释没有收录。除此之外，这部书收录的附录内容与彭嘉生译本大体上相同，但内容更丰富。

格尔到费尔巴哈》(*von Hegel bis Feuerbach*)①。

第七个译本是韬奋摘译的《费尔巴哈论》第四章的一个脚注，篇名为《恩格斯的自白》，载《读书偶译》。②

第八个译本，同时也是对新中国成立后翻译的《费尔巴哈论》影响最大的译本，是由张仲实先生翻译、生活书店于1937年12月出版的。这本书甫一出版就受到欢迎和关注，因此时隔不久（1938年2月）就在汉口再版。这个译本是全译文，而且附上了序言，还附录马克思《关于费尔巴哈的提纲》，书前有译者序言（写于1937年8月1日），以及《伟大的哲学家》和《费尔巴哈与新兴哲学》两篇介绍文章。这个版本是竖排平装本，书名定为《费尔巴哈论》，书的扉页上印有"世界名著译丛之二"字样。接下来，在1938年4月，上海书店仍以《费尔巴哈论》为名进行了再版。这个版本目前由上海图书馆收藏。

接近新中国成立时，即1949年9月，北京解放社重印，但注明的却是初版。这一版仍为竖排平装本，但书名已经改成了《费尔巴哈与德国古典哲学的终结》（仍是全译文），而且这个版本附上了序言和马克思的《费尔巴哈论纲》，书前有译者序言（写于1949年6月8日），文中有著者注、俄文版编者注和译者注。本版根据《马克思恩格斯文选》（两卷本）1948年俄文版重新校正。

在新中国成立后，这个版本不断出版，根据资料显示，在新中国成立之后至少出现过多个版本，都是以新中国成立前的译本为基础进行的再版。现对这些版本列举如下：

（1）在新中国成立之初，《费尔巴哈论》就在1949年11月出版了解放社上海版的竖排平装本。这个版本是根据1949年9月校正版重印的，本版现收藏于浙江省图书馆。（2）解放社于1949年11月出

---

① 参见《黑格尔哲学批判》，上海：辛垦书店1935年版，第172—189页。其中收录了费尔巴哈的《黑格尔哲学批判》，马克思的《黑格尔法律哲学批判导言》（即《黑格尔法哲学批判导言》）、《黑格尔辩证法及哲学一般之批判》（即《1844年经济学哲学手稿》中的《对黑格尔的辩证法和整个哲学的批判》）和《黑格尔现象学批判草案》，恩格斯的《关于黑格尔》和《从黑格尔到费尔巴哈》。

② 参见韬奋编译：《读书偶译》，上海：韬奋出版社1937年版，第119页。

版了大连版的竖排平装本，这个版本也是根据1949年9月校正版重印的，目前该版由中央编译局图书馆收藏。(3) 根据资料显示，北京人民出版社于1949年9月出版了《费尔巴哈与德国古典哲学的终结》（第一版），书后附有《译者后记》（写于1953年3月3日），书名根据《马克思恩格斯文选》（两卷本）俄文版校订，并经陈昌浩校阅。1954年8月，北京人民出版社出版了第二版。1957年10月，北京人民出版社第三版，尽管书名是《费尔巴哈与德国古典哲学的终结》，但书后附加上了65条注释和人名索引以及《普列汉诺夫为恩格斯〈费尔巴哈与德国古典哲学的终结〉一书俄译本所写的序言和注释》和《对普列汉诺夫译文的注释》，译者于1956年9月24日为第三版写了《中译本第三版校订后记》。(4) 1964年6月，人民出版社出版大字本的《费尔巴哈论》，共分为2册，为横排函装本，并于1965年1月改版，书名为《费尔巴哈与德国古典哲学的终结》，书后附注释（87条）和人名索引，以及《普列汉诺夫为恩格斯〈费尔巴哈与德国古典哲学的终结〉一书俄译本所写的序言和注释》，本书马恩著作部分是张仲实译，经中共中央编译局根据《马克思恩格斯全集》俄文第二版第21卷和第3卷做了一些校订，并采用了有关本书的注释，书后普列汉诺夫为本书俄译本缩写的序言和注释部分是由中共中央编译局根据《普列汉诺夫哲学著作选集》第1卷和《普列汉诺夫全集》第18卷俄文版译出的。

第九个译本是由曹真翻译、上海文源出版社于1949年10月出版的竖排平装本《费儿巴赫》，书后附上了马克思的《费儿巴赫论纲要》（即《关于费尔巴哈的提纲》），但是这个版本没有刊印恩格斯后来写的序言。

新中国成立前最后一个译本是著名文学家周建人摘译的版本，摘译的内容仅有第2章前半部分和第4章前半部分，篇名为《鲁德维息·费尔巴哈》，著者译为"恩格尔斯"。这个版本载于英·E.朋司编辑的《新哲学手册》（第6—19页）。

(二) 新中国成立以后《费尔巴哈论》的翻译出版

新中国成立后，为了更全面系统地传播马克思主义，巩固马克思主义指导思想的地位，中共中央于1953年成立了中央编译局，开始组织对马克思恩格斯等马克思主义经典作家著作的翻译、出版等工作。除了张仲实的译本在新中国成立后仍然在不断再版之外，还有一些版本值得注意。其中之一是集体翻译、唯真校订的《费尔巴哈与德国古典哲学的终结》，这个版本载于《马克思恩格斯文选》第2卷（1965年），并且附加上了序言。其二就是目前我们看到的《马克思恩格斯全集》中文版第一版。《马克思恩格斯全集》是在《马克思恩格斯全集》俄文版第二版的基础上翻译过来的，时间持续了将近30年（最早于1956年出版的《马克思恩格斯全集》第3卷至1985年出版的多个卷次）。①《费尔巴哈论》收录于1965年9月出版的《马克思恩格斯全集》第21卷，其中全面收录了《费尔巴哈和德国古典哲学的终结》的全文及其《序言》。这个版本是在张仲实的译本的基础上根据《马克思恩格斯全集》德文版第21卷校订的，校订时还参考了俄、英等译文和其他有关的中译文。

1972年4月，北京人民出版社出版了一个横排平装本，其中包括正文、序言以及马克思的《关于费尔巴哈的提纲》，后面还附上了33条注释以及几篇附录，其中包括：(1)《普列汉诺夫为恩格斯〈费尔巴哈与德国古典哲学的终结〉一书俄译本所写的序言和注释》，(2)《〈普列汉诺夫哲学著作选集〉俄文版编者为普列汉诺夫的序言和注释所加的注释》。最后是在1972年出版《马克思恩格斯选集》时，编选者把《费尔巴哈论》（包括序言在内）又收录其中。

新中国成立后除了上述中译本之外，民族出版社根据中共中央编译

---

① 相关资料参见中央编译局网站，http://www.cctb.net/wxzl/jd/maen/。

局的中译本翻译、出版了多个民族语言的版本,其中包括蒙文版(1975年3月)、藏文版(1980年4月)、维吾尔文版(1975年10月)、朝鲜文版(1974年10月)、哈萨克文版(1980年2月)等民族文字译本。内蒙古人民出版社于1957年4月出版蒙古人民共和国达什多尔吉译的蒙文译本。

尽管《费尔巴哈论》已经有多个版本,但新中国的编译和研究人员并没有停止对它进行完善。在这里有两个小例子可以证明国内马克思主义研究翻译人员在完善《费尔巴哈论》中译本上所做的努力。

第一个例子是关于"哲学的基本问题"及其相关内容之翻译的不断完善。众所周知,像《费尔巴哈论》这样的经典著作往往会有多个译本,通过对比能够发现,后来的译本整体上明显优于之前的译本。就拿"哲学的基本问题"的翻译来说,较早的林超真的译本是这样翻译的:"一切哲学尤其是近代哲学之根本大问题,就是关于思想和真实的关系问题,换一句话说,也就是精神和物质的关系问题。……那些认为物质——自然界——本来存在的哲学家就属于唯物论的各派。"① 张仲实的译本对这一内容的翻译如下:"一切哲学,特别是近代哲学的最重大的根本问题,便是思维对存在的关系问题。……凡承认自然界为基本东西的,则属于各种不同的唯物论。"② 目前我们最常见的译本是这样翻译的:"全部哲学,特别是近代哲学的重大的基本问题,是思维和存在的关系问题。……凡是认为自然界是本原的,则属于唯物主义的各种派别。"③ 正如人们所指出的那样,其中变化最为突出的是"本原"的翻译——它"从最初的'精神先存在',到后来的'精神'先于自然界

---

① 林超真编译:《宗教·哲学·社会主义》,上海:亚东图书馆1929年版,第299—301页。

② 《费尔巴哈和德国古典哲学的终结》,张仲实译,上海:解放社1949年版,第34—36页。

③ 《马克思恩格斯文集》第4卷,北京:人民出版社2009年版,第277—278页。

而存在，再到'精神对自然界来说是本原的'，这里显然……是概念意思上的改变。"① 这种术语的遴选和修改证明，《费尔巴哈论》的翻译已经达到了相当高度水准。

第二个例子是一篇整体讨论《费尔巴哈论》译本改动的文章——《〈费尔巴哈论〉译文的修改情况》②。中央编译局的编译人员所撰写《〈费尔巴哈论〉译文的修改情况》针对的是《马克思恩格斯选集》第4卷译文存在的两个主要问题：其一是对之前不确切的译文进行修订，其二是对原译文中遗留的俄文的表达方式进行了修订。③ 应该说，编译人员对以前译文中的一些不准确甚至错误的地方进行了校正，有些校正仅仅是字面上的修改，有一些则是根本性的改变。比如第一种情况，有这样一句话，"Ebensowenig wie die Erkenntnis kann die Geschichite einen vollendenden Abschluss finden in einem vollkommen Idealzustand der Menschheit"。这句话最初被译为："历史同认识一样，永远不会**把人类的某种完美的理想状态看作尽善尽美的**"，但这句话的真正内涵是："历史不会达到完美的理想状态而终结"，据此，他们把原译文改为"历史同认识一样，永远不会**在人类的一种完美的理想状态中结束**"。④

对于第二种情况，俄文译文在翻译过程中可能就存在着问题。比如："Die Menschen machen ihre Geschichte, wie diese auch immer ausfalle,

---

① 徐素华：《马克思恩格斯著作在中国的传播：MEGA² 视野下的文本、文献、语义学研究》，北京：中国社会科学出版社2013年版，第119—120页。在这部分，尽管我在查看到徐素华引用的几个译本之前已经注意到了这些区别，但本文在这里仍直接采用了徐素华的研究成果。
② 这篇文章作为附录收录于吴振海主编：《〈费尔巴哈论〉教程》，天津：天津人民出版社1987年版，第214—252页。此文最初发表于《马列著作编译资料》第2辑，北京：人民出版社1979年版。本书在这一部分基本上摘录的是这篇文章的内容。
③ 众所周知，《费尔巴哈论》的最初中译本是从俄文转译过来的。如果说我们像伽达默尔所说的那样认为文本具有不可译性，那么转译就会出现更多的问题。或许这就是人们强调要回到（原始）文本，并强调要以 MEGA² 来翻译《费尔巴哈论》的最根本原因。
④ 吴振海主编：《〈费尔巴哈论〉教程》，第246页；另参见《马克思恩格斯文集》第4卷，北京：人民出版社2009年版，第270页。

indem jeder seine eignen, bewusst gewollten Zwecke verfolgt, und die Resultante dieser vielen in verschiedenen Richtungen agierenden Willen und ihrer mannigfachen Einwirkung auf die Aussenwelt ist eben die Geschichte."这段话最初译为:"人们通过每一个人追求他自己的、自觉预期的目的而创造自己的历史,却不管这种历史的结局如何,而这许多按不同方向活动的愿望及其对外部世界的各种各样影响所产生的**结果**,就是历史。"后来编译组人员将之改译为:"无论历史的结局如何,人们总是通过每一个人追求他自己的、自觉预期的目的来创造他们的历史,而这许多按不同方向活动的愿望及其对外部世界的各种各样作用的**合力**,就是历史。"① 对于这句话,我们来看一看关键词"Einwirkung",如果将之译为"影响",从字面上看似乎也没有什么错误,但是如果将之译为"合力",那么这会解决人们对唯物史观的攻击,并处理好个人意志与历史规律之间的辩证关系。应该说,这是一个较好的处理方式。但是,这篇文章中的一些改译也有一些不尽如人意之处。比如:"Wie in Frankreich im achtzehenten, so leitete auch in Deutschland im neunzehnten Jahrhundert die philosophische Revolution den politischen Zusammenbruch ein."原文曾译为:"正像在十八世纪的法国一样,在十九世纪的德国,哲学革命也作了政治变革的前导",编译组成员将之改为:"正像在十八世纪的法国一样,在十九世纪的德国,哲学革命也作了政治崩溃的前导。"② 但是我们如果再考察一下最新的中译本就会发现,译文仍然保留了"政治变革"的译法。实际上,如果我们根据恩格斯文章的现实语境不难看出,"变革"仍然是一个更加恰当的译法。

---

① 参见吴振海主编:《〈费尔巴哈论〉教程》,第251—252页;《马克思恩格斯文集》第4卷,北京:人民出版社2009年版,第302页。
② 吴振海主编:《〈费尔巴哈论〉教程》,第251页;《马克思恩格斯文集》第4卷,第267页。现在的译文是:"正像在18世纪的法国一样,在19世纪的德国,哲学革命也作了政治变革的前导。"

(三)"Ausgang"的翻译问题:一个个案

《费尔巴哈论》的德文全称是: Ludwig Feuerbach und der Ausgang der klassischen deutschen Philosophie。尽管我们在上文已经提到了翻译人员对《费尔巴哈论》中很多核心思想和术语的翻译进行了反复斟酌,无疑,这对我们准确把握恩格斯的思想非常关键,但还有一个关键术语的翻译及其理解需要给予重点关注,那就是究竟如何翻译和理解恩格斯这篇论著之题目中的术语"Ausgang"。

根据《新德汉词典》,"Ausgang"的含义有8项之多,其中与《费尔巴哈论》相关的包括:"结果、结局","末端、尽头……(一个时期的)末尾、结束","出口、出口处"以及"开端、起点、出发点"等含义。在《费尔巴哈论》中,最贴近的含义应该是"(一个时期的)末尾、结束",这个时期可以理解为"德国古典哲学时期"。但是,如果认为恩格斯在使用"Ausgang"时仅指这个时期的结束,那么有一些问题是难以理解的,比如对黑格尔以及青年黑格尔派之思想的理解和评价问题。① 但从另外一个角度来看,这个术语毕竟还包含着另外一个含义——"开端、起点、出发点"。这是不是意味着,恩格斯是在指证费尔巴哈的唯物主义哲学为当时的哲学思想在思辨哲学领域内绕圈子指出了一条新的路向呢?这一点在《费尔巴哈论》的结尾处似乎能够得到

---

① 我们在恩格斯晚年的很多著作中都看到,对黑格尔以及马克思批判尤甚的布鲁诺·鲍威尔,恩格斯都给予了较高的(同时也是较为客观的)评价。对于黑格尔及其哲学的积极评价,我们在《费尔巴哈论》中就能够窥见一斑,比如他在直陈黑格尔及其哲学的巨大影响时指出:"可以理解,黑格尔的体系在德国的富有哲学味道的气氛中曾发生了多么巨大的影响。这是一次胜利进军,它延续了几十年,而且决没有随着黑格尔的逝世而停止。"(《马克思恩格斯文集》第4卷,北京:人民出版社2009年版,第273页。) 其中,我们还看到了恩格斯对青年黑格尔派的褒扬。除此之外,恩格斯还专门撰文赞扬鲍威尔在思想领域中的革命性作用。在1882年4月份撰写的《布鲁诺·鲍威尔和早期基督教》一文中,恩格斯对鲍威尔的历史价值和地位给予了较高的评价,他认为,尽管人们(即官方神学家)对鲍威尔的逝世持有一种冷漠的态度,但后者"比所有这些人更有价值"。因为在解决早期基督教如何能够产生并取得历史统治地位,并使之从一个被压迫阶级的宗教转变为"罗马世界专制皇帝的最好手段"问题上,"布鲁诺·鲍威尔的贡献比任何人大得多",尽管这些研究仍然存在这样或那样的问题。参见《马克思恩格斯全集》第19卷,北京:人民出版社1963年版,第327—329页。

佐证，因为恩格斯在那里指出，在"有教养的"阶级抛弃理论转向实践的过程中，德国人似乎失去了理论兴趣。但在他看来，"德国人的理论兴趣，只是在工人阶级中还没有衰退，继续存在着。在这里，它是根除不了的"。而且只有德国的工人阶级及其主导的社会运动才是真正的"德国古典哲学的继承者"。① 在某种意义上，德国古典哲学在终结的地方直接指向了另外一个出路，那就是马克思主义。

但是在翻译过程中，由于理解上的问题，各种版本的不同译法却导致了各种误解。比如在英文版中，较为流行的译本对"Ausgang"的就有两种译法，一种是译为"Outcome"（结果、成果），另外一种就是"End"（终结、目的）。但是，《马克思恩格斯全集》中文版在翻译这个术语时，基本上采取的是第二种译法，即将"Ausgang"译为"终结"。然而，这种翻译却最终导致了人们对马克思和恩格斯对待德国古典哲学甚至是对哲学的态度产生了误解。因为，根据后一种译法，德国哲学（尤其是思辨的观念论哲学）随着马克思主义的出现已然消亡，从此以后再没有哲学可言。

正是为了矫正上述翻译所带来的理解上的误解，所以一些专业的哲学家兼翻译家才主张重新理解这个术语，矫正以前的翻译。贺麟先生即为一例。根据他的回忆，中央编译局和中央党校专门就《费尔巴哈论》的翻译修改召开了一个研讨会，他在会上指出，"Ausgang""译为'出发'或'出路'比较合适"，他的理由除了"Ausgang"的本义外，还有两个文本上的证明，其一是"至于费尔巴哈，虽然他在好些方面是黑格尔哲学和我们的观点之间的中间环节"；其二是"在这种情况下，我感到越来越有必要把我们同黑格尔哲学的关系，我们怎样从这一哲学出发又怎样同它脱离，作一个简要而又系统的阐述"。② 贺麟先生指出，根据恩格斯的论述，费尔巴哈在黑格尔哲学和马克思主义哲学之间作为中间环节确实起到了重要作用。既然是中间环节，那么题中应有之义

---

① 《马克思恩格斯文集》第4卷，北京：人民出版社2009年版，第312—313页。
② 《马克思恩格斯文集》第4卷，北京：人民出版社2009年版，第265—266页。

是，它既非某个理论体系的开端，也不是一个理论的终结点，它仅仅是为某个走到穷途末路的哲学找到一个桥梁。① 不难看出，贺麟先生的理解与恩格斯的解释是一致的。

如果将贺麟先生的观点加以拓展和具体化，那么对于费尔巴哈来说，他在以黑格尔为核心的德国古典哲学中确实起到了桥梁作用，因为当思辨哲学在面对幽暗闭塞的社会现实面前而无所作为时，就必须寻找另外一个出路。找到这个出路的人，恩格斯看来，就是费尔巴哈，而这个出路，就是他的"唯物主义"。如若要把"Ausgang"翻译为"终结"，那么这种"终结"也仅仅是针对以黑格尔哲学为代表的思辨哲学的"终结"，而不是整个西方哲学思想，甚至不是其他哲学体系的终结。② 但对于西方哲学中的其他哲学流派来说，费尔巴哈甚至对其产生和发展没有产生任何影响。③

也许正是认识到了这一点。朱光潜先生才提出了与贺麟先生译法不同、内涵一致的译法，即"结果"或"成果"。朱先生也通过马克思恩格斯的文献指出，把"Ausgang"译为"终结"或"终点"的译法显然没有充分考察到原作者的意图，因为不管是在马克思的《资本论》中，还是在《费尔巴哈论》中，都不能让马克思和恩格斯的理论达到内在的一致性。朱光潜进而指出，英、法、俄等译本对"Ausgang"的翻译都不准确，中文更是以讹传讹。在"1962年柏林德国科学院新出版的多卷本《现代德语大词典》"中，在例证"Ausgang"的第44项的含义时，列举的就是恩格斯的《费尔巴哈论》，在这里它的含义是"一个时间段落"，同时通过对照1964年出版的马克思的《1844年经济学哲

---

① 中央编译局马克思恩格斯室编：《马克思恩格斯著作在中国的传播》，北京：人民出版社1983年版，第176—177页。

② 我们在下文将会指出，就算是费尔巴哈，也没有完全"终结"黑格尔派哲学或"唯心主义"，因为他在实践领域仍然在继续坚持"唯心主义"。这也是马克思恩格斯批判费尔巴哈"半截子唯物主义"的原因之一。

③ 比如，费尔巴哈同时代的叔本华和尼采的意志论哲学甚至之后的现象学等都仍然在西方哲学传统中占据着重要甚至是主流位置。

学手稿》的译本，得出了译为"结果"或"成果"更为合理的结论。①尽管这种译法也具有一定的模糊性——在中文当中，人们很少将"结果"或"成果"理解为阶段性的，而是一般将之理解为结论性的——但这毕竟肯定了德国古典哲学的价值和意义，因而也为开放性理解它留下了空间。

通过"Ausgang"的翻译不难看出，包括《费尔巴哈论》在内的马克思恩格斯著述的中文译本在翻译者和研究专家的努力下变得越来越准确可信。所以我们有理由相信，随着整体编译水平的提高，人们不再经过转译（主要是经过俄文版和日文版等），而是越来越直接面对最初乃至最原始的文本——《马克思恩格斯全集》中文第二版基本上是依据原文（即最权威的版本 MEGA²）翻译过来的——所以《马克思恩格斯全集》第二版的翻译应该是值得信赖的，当然前提是在翻译过程中必须充分借鉴前人的研究、翻译成果。当然，由于收录《费尔巴哈论》的 MEGA² 第 I 部门第 30 卷刚刚于 2011 年出版，《马克思恩格斯全集》第二版还没有翻译和出版这一文献，所以未来是值得期待的。②

（本文来自 2016 年中央编译出版社出版的田毅松所著《恩格斯〈路德维希·费尔巴哈和德国古典哲学的终结〉研究读本》有关内容。）

---

① 关于马克思，这里指的是他在《资本论》第 1 卷第二版的跋中对黑格尔及其哲学的尊重和强调——"我公开承认我是这位大思想家的学生，并且在关于价值理论的一章中，有些地方我甚至卖弄起黑格尔特有的表达方式。辩证法在黑格尔手中神秘化了，但这决没有妨碍他第一个全面地有意识地叙述了辩证法的一般运动形式。"（《马克思恩格斯文集》第 5 卷，北京：人民出版社 2009 年版，第 22 页）关于恩格斯，指的则是在《费尔巴哈论》结尾处的论断——"德国的工人运动是德国古典哲学的继承者。"（《马克思恩格斯文集》第 4 卷，北京：人民出版社 2009 年版，第 313 页。朱光潜：《美学拾穗集》，北京：百花文艺出版社 1980 年版，第 43—44 页。）

② 值得注意的是，尽管有些版本在 MEGA² 中已经有了最新版本，但这些最新成果在最新翻译的马克思恩格斯文献中并没有体现出来。比如《资本论》及其手稿在 MEGA² 中作为一个部门单独列出，并且已经完全出齐，然而有的学者指出，不管是《马克思恩格斯全集》第二版的第 44—46 卷，还是《马克思恩格斯文集》第 5—7 卷，都没有吸收 MEGA² 的编辑成果。

FEUERBACH

THE ROOTS OF THE SOCIALIST PHILOSOPHY

BY

FREDERICK ENGELS

TRANSLATED WITH CRITICAL INTRODUCTION

BY

AUSTIN LEWIS

CHICAGO
CHARLES H. KERR & COMPANY

Copyright, 1903
By CHARLES H. KERR & COMPANY

CONTENTS

Introduction ································ 3
Author's Preface ························ 33
Feuerbach
    I ···································· 37
    II ··································· 56
    III ·································· 76
    IV ··································· 92
Appendix ································· 129

INTRODUCTION.

This work takes us back nearly sixty years, to a time when what is now a movement of universal significance was in its infancy. Hegel and the Revolution of 1848; these are the points of departure. To the former, we owe the philosophic form of the socialist doctrine, to the latter, its practical activity as a movement.

In the midst of the turmoil and strife and apparent defeat of those days two men, Marx and Engels, exiled and without influence, betook themselves to their books and began laboriously to fashion the form and doctrine of the most powerful intellectual and political movement of all time. To the task they brought genius, scholarship, and a capacity for hard work and patient research. In each of these qualities they were supreme. Marx possessed a colossal mind; no thinker upon social subjects, not even Herbert Spencer, has been his superior, for the lonely socialist could claim a comprehensiveness, a grasp of relations and a

INTRODUCTION

power of generalization, together with a boldness of conception, which place him in a class by himself. Engels was the able co-adjutor and co-worker with Marx. He was a deep and acute thinker, a most patient investigator, a careful writer. More practical than his friend, he was better able to cope with material problems, and his advice and his purse were always at the disposal of Marx.

The latter could hardly have worked under more discouraging conditions. Poverty, inadequate opportunities, lack of stimulating companionship, and the complete absence of any kind of encouragement and such sympathy as a man of his affectionate temperament craved fell to his lot. His most learned works were written for groups of workingmen, his most laborious efforts were made without the slightest hope of recognition from the learned and the powerful.

All through these years Engels remained his faithful friend, and helped him over many hard places when family troubles and straitened circumstances pressed upon the old revolutionist.

INTRODUCTION

This work is Engels' testimony with regard to the method employed by them in arriving at their philosophical conclusions. It is the statement of the philosophical foundations of modern socialism by one who helped to lay them; it is an old man's account of the case upon the preparation of which he has spent his entire life, for, this work, short as it is, represents the results of forty years of toil and persevering effort.

As the "Communist Manifesto" was a gage flung with all the impetuosity of youthful impatience into the face of constituted authority, so this is the deliberate statement of the veteran, who has learned the game too well to leave any openings, and proceeds to the demolition of pet opinions in a quiet, deadly and deliberate fashion.

Step by step, the argument is built up. The ghosts of old controversies long since buried are raised, to show how the doctrine imperishably associated with the names of Marx and Engels came into existence; the "Young Hegelians," the "Tuebingen School," and finally Feuerbach himself are

INTRODUCTION

summoned from the grave to which the Revolution of 1848 had consigned them. Still, ancient history as these controversies are from the German standpoint, such is the backwardness of philosophy among English-speaking peoples, that we find Engels exposing again and again fallacies which persist even in our time, and ridiculing sentiments which we receive with approbation in our political assemblies, and with mute approval in our churches and conventicles.

The anti-religious note is noticeable throughout, in itself an echo of controversies long past, when the arguments of the critics of the Bible were creating now fury, now dismay, throughout Christendom, before the Higher Criticism had become respected, and before soi-disant sceptics could continue to go solemnly to church.

Moreover, the work was written in German for German workmen for whom religion has not the same significance as it apparently still continues to possess for the English-speaking people, whose sensitiveness upon the subject appears to have outlived their faith. However that may be,

INTRODUCTION

religious bodies possess a curious and perhaps satisfactory faculty of absorbing the truths of science, and still continuing to exist, and even to thrive, upon what the inexperienced might easily mistake for a deadly diet.

Under the circumstances there is no reason why Engels' remarks should affect even the timorous, although it must be remembered that a very able English socialist philosopher is reputed to have damaged his chances irretrievably by an ill-judged quotation from Mr. Swinburne.

It must be confessed that the occasional bitterness in which Engels indulges is to be deplored, in a work of so essentially intellectual a character, but it is little to be wondered at. His contempt for university professors and the pretentious cultivated classes, who claim so much upon such slight grounds, is not strange, when we consider the honest labors of himself and his colleagues and the superficial place-hunting of the recognized savants. He loves learning for its own sake, for the sake of truth and scientific accuracy, and he cannot

INTRODUCTION

feel anything but scorn for those who use it as a means to lull the consciences of the rich, and to gain place and power for themselves. The degradation of German philosophy affects him with a real sorrow; the scholar is outraged at the mockery. "Sterility," "eclecticism," these are the terms in which he sums up the teachings of the official professors, and they are almost too gentle to be applied to the dispiriting and disheartening doctrines which are taught to the English-speaking student of to-day under the name of economics or philosophy.

In the first part of his pamphlet, for it is little more in size, Engels gives a short and concise account of the work of Hegel and the later Hegelian School. He shows how the philosophy of Hegel has both a conservative and a radical side and how conservatives and radicals alike might, (as a matter of fact they did), each derive support from his teachings, according to the amount of stress laid respectively upon the great divisions of his work, the "System" and the "Dialectic."

INTRODUCTION

The Extreme Left developed through the application of the dialectic, and applied the philosophic doctrine thus derived to the criticism of existing political and religious institutions. This resulted in the gradual throwing away of the abstract part of the Hegelian philosophy, and in the study of facts and phenomena to an ever-increasing degree.

Marx had, in his youth, allied himself with the "Young Hegelians," as this school was called, and this fact had no slight influence upon his subsequent career. His critics lay the blame for much of the obscurity of language from which "Capital" in particular suffers, at the door of this training. His painful elaboration of thesis, antithesis, and synthesis, his insistence upon the dialectic, and his continual use of the Hegelian philosophical expressions are due to his earlier controversial experiences. Still, on the other hand, his patient investigation of actual facts, his insistence on the value of positive knowledge as compared with abstract theory, and his diligent and persistent use of blue-books and statis-

INTRODUCTION

tics, were in a great measure results of the same training.

Now and again, we find Engels in this work displaying remarkable controversial acumen, as in his discussion of the phrase, "All that is real is reasonable, and all that is reasonable is real" (Alles was wirklich ist, ist vernuenftig, und alles was vernuenftig ist, ist wirklich). From this expression, by the development of the Hegelian argument, he arrives at the conclusion involved in the statement that the value of a social or political phenomenon is its transitoriness, the necessity of its disappearance. Hence the abolition of dogmatic statement and mere subjective reasoning in the realm of philosophy, the destruction of the old school of which Kant was the chief exponent, and the creation of a new school the most advanced teachers of which were, as they still are, the materialistic socialists, of whom Engels and Marx are the chief.

The object of this historical sketch is to show the origin of Feuerbach's philosophy as well as of that of Marx and Engels. As the fight between the Young Hegelians and

INTRODUCTION

the conservatives grew hotter, the radicals were driven back upon the English-French materialism of the preceding century. This was embarrassing for followers of Hegel, who had been taught to regard the material as the mere expression of the Idea. Feuerbach relieved them from the contradiction. He grasped the question boldly and threw the Hegelian abstraction completely to one side. His book, "Wesen des Christenthums," in which his ideas were set forth, became immediately popular, and an English translation, which was widely read, was made of it by George Eliot under the title of "Essence of Christianity."

Engels is by no means grudging of expressions of appreciation with regard to this work, and its effects both upon himself and the educated world in general. This "unendurable debt of honor" paid, however, he proceeds to attack the idealistic humanitarianism which Feuerbach had made the basis and sanction of his ethical theories.

Although Feuerbach had arrived at the materialistic conclusion, he expressed him-

INTRODUCTION

self as unable to accept materialism as a doctrine. He says that as far as the past is concerned he is a materialist, but, for the future, he is not so—"Backward I am in agreement with the materialists, forward not"—a statement which impels Engels to examine the materialism of the eighteenth century, which he finds purely mechanical, without any conception of the universe as a process, and therefore utterly inadequate for the philosophic needs of the period at which Feuerbach wrote; for by that time the advance of science, and the greater powers of generalization, arising from patient experimentation, and the development of the evolutionary theory, had rendered the eighteenth century views evidently absurd.

The "vulgarising peddlers (vulgarisirenden Hausirer) come in for a great deal of contempt at the hands of Engels. These were the popular materialists—"the blatant atheists," who, without scientific knowledge and gifted with mere oratory or a popular style of writing, used every advance of science as a weapon of attack upon the Creator and popular religion. Engels sneers

INTRODUCTION

at these as not being scientists at all, but mere tradesmen dealing in pseudo-scientific wares. He calls their occupation a trade, a business (Geschaeft). Of the same class was that host of secularist lecturers who at one time thronged the lecture platforms of the English-speaking countries and of whom Bradlaugh and Ingersoll were in every way the best representatives. These secularists have now ceased to exercise any influence, and the Freethought societies, at one time so numerous, have now practically disappeared. In accordance with the theories as set forth by Engels they were bound to disappear; their teachings had no real bearing upon social progress, they contributed nothing of any scientific value to modern thought, and as Engels carefully shows, the reading of history by these lecturers was vitiated by a lack of scientific grasp, and inability to take a rational view of the great principles of historical development.

In the third part of this little book Engels deals with a very interesting question which still disturbs the minds of philosophers, and concerning which much discussion goes

INTRODUCTION

on even among the materialists; that is the question as to the effect of religion upon social progress. Feuerbach had made the statement that periods of social progress are marked by religious changes. He uses religion as a synonym for human love, forcing the meaning of the word religion from the Latin "religare," "to tie," in order to give it an etymological and derivative meaning in support of his statement, a controversial trick for which he is rebuked by Engels. The declaration that great historical revolutions are accompanied by religious changes is declared by Engels not to be true, except in a limited degree as regards the three great world-religions—Christianity, Mahommedanism and Buddhism.

Engels declared that the change in religion simultaneous with economic and political revolution stopped short with the bourgeois revolt which was made without any appeal to religion whatsoever. It is evident that this is not entirely true, for in the English-speaking countries, at all events, not only the bourgeois but frequently also

INTRODUCTION

the proletarian movements attempt to justify themselves from Scripture. The teachings of the Bible and the Sermon on the Mount are frequently called to the aid of the revolutionary party; Christian Socialists, in the English and American, not the continental sense of the term, as such are admitted to the International Congresses; and other evidences of the compatibility of religion with the proletarian movement can be traced.

But in the broader sense of his statement Engels is undoubtedly correct. The proletarian movement, unlike that of the bourgeois, has produced no definite religious school, it has not claimed any particular set of religious doctrines as its own. As a matter of fact, there appears to be an ever-widening chasm between the Church and the laborer, a condition of affairs which is freqently deplored in religious papers. The famous Papal Encyclical on Labor was certainly intended to retain the masses in the Church, and the formation of trades unions under the influence of the priests was a logical conclusion from the teachings of the

INTRODUCTION

Papal Encyclical. But such religious movements are in no sense representative of the working-class movement; in fact they are resented and antagonized by the regular proletarian movement which proceeds under the leadership of the Socialists.

Feuerbach's exaltation of humanitarianism, as a religion, is derided by Engels in a semi-jocular, semi-serious manner, for his statement that Feuerbach's ideals can be completely realized on the Bourse, cannot be taken seriously. Engels' clear-sightedness with regard to the ineffectiveness of a purely humanitarian religion is very remarkable, although the forty years' additional experience which he had over Feuerbach was a great advantage to him in estimating the actual value of humanitarian religion as an influence in human affairs. Since the time of Feuerbach various experiments in the direction of a religion based entirely on Love have been tried, and none of them has succeeded. Positivism or its religious side has been a failure. It has appealed to a small set of men, some of whom are possessed of great ability and

INTRODUCTION

have accomplished much, but as a religion in any adequate sense of the word positivism will be admitted a failure by its most sincere adherents. Brotherhood Churches, the Church of Humanity, the People's Church, and other like organizations have been formed having the same humanitarian basis, professing to cultivate a maximum of love with a minimum of faith, and have failed to impress ordinary men and women. Theosophy, a system of oriental mysticism based on an abstract conception of the brotherhood of man, has also put forth its claims to notice, on the grounds of its broad humanitarianism. None of these humanitarian religions, however, appear to satisfy the needs of the times, which do not seem to demand any humanitarian teachings. The only religions which evidently persist are the dogmatic, those appealing undisguisedly to faith, and even these do not maintain their proletarian following.

Engels' remarks appear to be more than justified by the facts of to-day, for so far from the proletarian forming a new religion representing his needs on the ideological"

INTRODUCTION

field, he appears to be increasingly desirous of releasing himself from the bands of any religion whatever, and substituting in place of it practical ethics and the teachings of science. Thus we are informed that five out of six of the working classes of Berlin, who attend any Sunday meetings whatever, are to be found in the halls of the Social Democratic Party, listening to the lectures provided by that organization.

The revolutionary character of Feuerbach's philosophy is not maintained in his ethic, which Engels declares with much truth to be no better than that of his predecessors, as the basis on which it stands is no more substantial. Feuerbach fails as a teacher of practical ethics; he is smothered in abstraction and cannot attain to any reality.

With the last part of the work Engels abandons the task of criticising Feuerbach, and proceeds to expound his own philosophy.

With absolute candor and modesty he gives Marx credit for the theory of the materialistic conception of history, upon the

INTRODUCTION

enunciation and proof of which he had himself worked almost incessantly ever since the first idea of the theory had occurred to them, forty years prior to the time when he wrote this work. The footnote to the first page of the fourth part is the testimony of a collaborator to the genius of his fellow-workman, an example of appreciation and modest self-effacement which it would not be easy to match, and to which literary men who work together are not over-prone. Nothing else could bear more eloquent testimony to the loftiness of character and sincerity of purpose of these two exiles.

The Marxian philosophy of history is clearly stated, and so fully explained by Engels that there is no need to go over the ground again, and there only remains to call attention to some of the modern developments in the direction of rigidity of interpretation, and to the exaggeration of the broad theory of the predominance of the economic factor into a hard and fast doctrine of economic determinism.

When we examine the claims of Engels on behalf of the materialistic doctrine it

INTRODUCTION

will be found that they are not by any means of such a nature as to warrant the extreme conclusions of subsequent socialist publicists and leaders. It must be remembered that the subject of the influence of economic conditions on religious and political phenomena has been closely examined of late years and continual and accumulating evidence has been forthcoming respecting the remarkable influence of economic facts upon all other manifestations of social activity. It is very probable that the successful investigations in this new field have led, temporarily, to the formation of exaggerated ideas as to the actual value of the economic factor.

Marx, in one of his short critical notes on Feuerbach, says: "The materialistic doctrine that men are products of conditions and education, different men therefore products of other conditions, and a different kind of education, forgets that circumstances may be altered by man and that the educator has himself to be educated." In other words, the problem, like all problems, possesses at least two quantities; it is not a question solely of conditions, economic or otherwise; it is a question of man and con-

INTRODUCTION

ditions, for the man is never dissolved in the conditions, but exists as a separate entity, and these two elements, man and conditions, act and react the one upon the other.

This is quite a different position from that taken by Lafargue in his fight with Jaures. Lafargue there argued that economic development is the sole determinant of progress, and pronounces in favor of economic determinism, thus reducing the whole of history and, consequently, the dominating human motives to but one elementary motive. Belfort Bax, the well-known English socialist writer, makes a very clever argument against the determinist position by comparing it with the attempts of the pre-Socratic Greek philosophers to reduce nature to one element. His remarks are so pertinent that a brief abstract of his argument is here quoted in his own language. He says in "Outlooks from a New Standpoint":

"The endeavor to reduce the whole of Human life to one element alone, to reconstruct all history on the basis of Economics,

INTRODUCTION

as already said, ignores the fact that every concrete reality must have a material and a formal side,—that is, it must have at least two ultimate elements—all reality as opposed to abstraction consisting in a synthesis. The attempt to evolve the many-sidedness of Human life out of one of its factors, no matter how important that factor may be, reminds one of the attempts of the early pre-Socratic Greeks to reduce nature to one element, such as water, air, fire, etc.''

And again:

''The precise form a movement takes, be it intellectual, ethical or artistic, I fully admit, is determined by the material circumstances of the society in which it acquires form and shape, but it is also determined by those fundamental psychological tendencies which have given it birth.''

Enrico Ferri, the famous Italian member of the Chamber of Deputies and criminologist, appears to be at one with Bax in this matter. He says, quoting from a recent translation of his ''Socialism and Modern Science'': ''It is perfectly true that every phenomenon as well as every in-

INTRODUCTION

stitution—moral, juridicial or political—is simply the result of the economic phenomena and the conditions of the transitory, physical and historical environments. But as a consequence of that law of natural causality which tells us that every effect is always the resultant of numerous concurrent causes, and not of one cause alone, and that every effect becomes in its turn a cause of other phenomena, it is necessary to amend and complete the too rigid form that has been given to this true idea.

"Just as all psychical manifestations of the individual are the result of the organic conditions (temperament) and of the environment in which he lives, in the same way, all the social manifestations of a people are the resultant of their organic conditions (race) and of the environment, as these are the determining causes of the given economic organization which is the physical basis of life."

These may be said to be fairly representative of the views of the opposition to the extreme of economic determinism.

The whole controversy has spread over a

INTRODUCTION

tremendous amount of ground and involves much reading. Some of the chief results have lately been summarized by Professor Seligman in his "Economic Interpretation of History." (Macmillan, 1902.) His written views show a closer approximation to and understanding of the teachings of the socialist philosophy on this subject than we have been accustomed to receive at the hands of official savants, so that it would seem as if the value of Marx's work was at last beginning to be appreciated even in the foggy studies of the professors. Two extracts from the writings of Engels are quoted by Professor Seligman. These extracts apparently go to prove that Engels by no means contemplated the extreme construction which has been placed upon the doctrine, and that he would find such a construction inconsistent with his general views.

These extracts are quoted here for the purpose of further elucidating the views of Engels and as further explanatory of the position assumed by him in the last part of the work under consideration.

INTRODUCTION

They form part of a series of articles writen for the "Sozialistische Akademiker" in 1890, and are as follows:

"Marx and I are partly responsible for the fact that the younger men have sometimes laid more stress on the economic side than it deserves. In meeting the attacks of our opponents it was necessary for us to emphasize the dominant principle denied by them, and we did not always have the time, place, or opportunity to let the other factors which were concerned in the mutual action and reaction get their deserts."

And in another letter to the same magazine he says: "According to the materialistic view of history, the factor which is, in last instance, decisive in history is the production and reproduction of actual life. More than this neither Marx nor I have ever asserted. But when anyone distorts this so as to read that the economic factor is the sole element he converts the statement into a meaningless, abstract, absurd phrase. The economic condition is the basis, but the various elements of the superstructure—the political forms of the class-

INTRODUCTION

contests, and their results, the constitutions —the legal forms and also all the reflexes of these actual contests in the brains of the participants, the political, legal, philosophical theories, the religious views—all these exert an influence on the development of the historical struggles, and in many instances determine their form.''

Here we may leave this much disputed matter for the present, as any involved discussion of controversial questions would be out of place here. The question in its ultimate form is merely scholastic, for not even the most extreme determinist would hold that only the economic argument must be relied upon by the orators and the press of the proletarian movement. Any one, however, who wishes to pursue the subject farther can find abundant material in the already great and growing amount of literature in connection with it.

There is no doubt that the ideas of Marx respecting the basis of historical progress have already revolutionized the teaching of history in the universities, although but few professors have been honest enough to give

INTRODUCTION

him credit for it. The economic factor continually acquires greater importance in the eyes of the student of history, but the practical discoverer of this factor is still slighted and the results of his labors are assimilated with a self-satisfied hypocrisy which is, unfortunately, characteristic of the colleges of the English-speaking countries.

The bourgeois writers upon socialism generally content themselves with the bold statement that Marx employs the dialectic method of investigation and statement. This is so much Greek to the ordinary reader, and the subject of the dialectic as used by socialist writers requires a few words of explanation.

The first part of this work is very valuable, therefore, as showing what Marx and Engels meant when they used the expression, and as declaring their estimation of that method compared with that in general use in their day, and always, prior to their time, employed in philosophy, history and economics.

A fuller and more detailed definition of the dialectic as applied by Engels is given

INTRODUCTION

by that philosopher in his famous reply to Eugene Duhring known as the "Umwaelzung der Wissenschaft." In that work a more thorough and patient investigation is made into the sources of materialistic philosophy of the socialist movement, for the reputation of his antagonist appears to have acted as a spur to Engels' faculties which certainly never showed to better advantage than in that work. A portion of the argument, in fact an abstract of the general train of reasoning, with the omission of the more obviously controversial parts, has been reprinted under the title of "Socialism from Utopia to Science." The following quotation is taken from the translation prepared for the "People" in 1892:

"We also find, upon a closer enquiry, that the two poles of an antithesis, such as positive and negative, are as inseparable from as they are opposed to each other, and that, despite their antagonism, they mutually pervade each other; and in the same way we find cause and effect to be conceptions whose force exists only when applied to a single instance, but which, soon as we con-

INTRODUCTION

sider that instance in its connection with the cosmos, run into each other and dissolve in the contemplation of that universal action and reaction where cause and effect constantly change places—that which is effect, now and here, becoming, then and yonder, cause, and vice versa.

"None of these processes and methods of reasoning fits in the metaphysical framework of thought. To dialectics, however, which takes in the objects and their conceivable images above all in their connections, their sequence, their motion, their rise and decline, processes like the above are so many attestations of its own method of procedure. Nature furnishes the test to dialectics, and this much we must say for modern natural science, that it has contributed towards this test an extremely rich and daily increasing material, whereby it has demonstrated that, in the last instance, nature proceeds upon dialectical, not upon metaphysical methods, that it does not move upon the eternal sameness of a perpetually recurring circle, but that it goes through an actual historic evolution.

INTRODUCTION

"This new German philosophy culminated in the system of Hegel. There for the first time—and herein consists its merit—the whole natural, historic, and intellectual world was presented as a process, i. e., engaged in perpetual motion, change, transformation and development. Viewed from this standpoint, the history of mankind no longer appeared as a wild tangle of senseless deeds of violence, all equally to be rejected by a ripened philosophic judgment, and which it were best to forget as soon as possible, but as the process of the development of mankind itself—a development whose gradual march, through all its stray paths, and its eternal law, through all its seeming fortuitousness, it now became the task of the intellect to trace and to discover."

Kirkup, in his "History of Socialism," has this to say upon the dialectic method of investigation as used by Marx: "In the system of Marx, it means that the business of enquiry is to trace the connection and concatenation in the links that make up the process of historic evolution, to investigate

INTRODUCTION

how one stage succeeds another in the development of society, the facts and forms of human life and history not being stable and stereotyped things, but the ever-changing manifestations of the fluent and unresting real, the course of which it is the duty of science to reveal.''

The translator has endeavored to render the meaning of the original in as simple an English form as possible, and to, generally speaking, avoid technical terms.

Austin Lewis.

AUTHOR'S PREFACE.

In the preface of the "Critique of Political Economy," published at Berlin, in 1859, Marx explained how we two, in 1845, in Brussels, intended to work out together the antagonism of our views—that is, the materialistic philosophy of history, as developed by Marx—to the ideological German philosophy, and, in fact, to compare it with our present philosophic knowledge. The design was carried out in the form of a criticism of post-Hegelian philosophy. The manuscript, two big octavo volumes, had long been at its intended place of publication in Westphalia, when we received the news that altered circumstances did not permit of its being printed. We postponed the publication of the manuscript indefinitely, all the more willingly, as we had attained our main object. an understanding of our own position.

AUTHOR'S PREFACE

Since then more than forty years have elapsed, and Marx has died without either of us having had an opportunity of coming back to the antithesis. As regards our position with reference to Hegel, we have explained that, as occasion has arisen, but, nowhere, as a whole. We never came back to Feuerbach, who occupies an intermediate position between the philosophy of Hegel and our own.

In the meantime the Marxian philosophy has found champions beyond the boundaries of Germany and of Europe, and in all the languages of the civilized world. On the other hand, the classic German philosophy has had a sort of new-birth abroad, particularly in England and Scandinavia, and even in Germany they appear to be substituting the thin soup of eclecticism which seems to flow from the universities under the name of philosophy.

Under these circumstances a short, compact explanation of our relations to the Hegelian philosophy, of our going forth and departure from it, appears to me to be more and more required. And just in the

AUTHOR'S PREFACE

same way a full recognition of the influence which Feuerbach, more than all the other post-Hegelian philosophers, had over us, during the period of our youthful enthusiasm, presents itself to me as an unendurable debt of honor. I also seize the opportunity the more readily since the editor of the "Neue Zeit" has asked me for a critical discussion of Starcke's book on Feuerbach. My work was published in the fourth and fifth volumes of 1886 of that publication and here appears in a revised special edition.

Before sending this manuscript to press I once again hunted up and examined the old manuscript of 1845-6. The part of it dealing with Feuerbach is not complete. The portion completed consists in an exposition of the materialistic view of history and only proves how incomplete at that time was our knowledge of economic history. The criticism of Feuerbach's doctrine is not given in it. It was therefore unsuitable for our purpose. On the other hand, I have found in an old volume of Marx the eleven essays on Feuerbach printed here as an ap-

AUTHOR'S PREFACE

pendix. These are notes hurriedly scribbled in for later elaboration, not in the least degree prepared for the press, but invaluable, as the first written form, in which is planted the genial germ of the new philosophy.   F<small>RIEDRICH</small> E<small>NGELS</small>.

London, 21 February, 1888.

FEUERBACH

I.

The volume before us brings us at once to a period which, in the matter of time, lies a full generation behind us, but which is as foreign to the present generation in Germany as if it were quite a century old. And, still, it was the period of the preparation of Germany for the revolution of 1848, and all that has happened to us since is only a continuation of 1848, only a carrying out of the last will and testament of the revolution.

Just as in France in the eighteenth, so in Germany in the nineteenth century, revolutionary philosophic conceptions introduced a breaking up of existing political conditions. But how different the two appear! The French were engaged in open fight with all recognized science, with the Church, frequently also with the State, their writings

FEUERBACH

were published beyond the frontiers in Holland or in England, and they themselves were frequently imprisoned in the Bastile. The Germans, on the contrary, were professors, appointed instructors of youth by the State, their writings, recognized text-books, and their definite system of universal progress, the Hegelian, raised, as it were, to the rank of a royal Prussian philosophy of government. And behind these professors, behind their pedantically obscure utterances, in their heavy wearisome periods, was it possible that the revolution could conceal itself? Were not just the people who were looked upon at that time as the leaders of the revolution, the Liberals, the bitterest opponents of the brain-turning philosophy? But what neither the Governmentalists nor the Liberals saw, that saw, at least one man, and that man was Heinrich Heine.

Let us take an example. No philosophic statement has so invited the thanks of narrow-minded governments and the anger of the equally narrow Liberals as the famous statement of Hegel: "All that is real is reasonable, and all that is reasonable is real."

FEUERBACH

This was essentially the blessing of all that is, the philosophical benediction of despotism, police-government, star-chamber justice and the censorship. So Frederick William III and his subjects understood it; but, according to Hegel, not everything which exists is, without exception, real. The attribute of reality belongs only to that which is at the same time necessary. Reality proves itself in the course of its development as necessity. Any governmental act —Hegel himself instances the example of a certain "tax law"—by no means strikes him as real in the absence of other qualities. But what is necessary proves itself in the last instance as reasonable also, and applied to the Prussian government, the Hegel doctrine, therefore, only means, this state is reasonable, corresponding with reason, as long as it is necessary, and if it appear to us an evil, but in spite of the evil still continues to exist, the evil of the government finds its justification and its explanation in the corresponding evil of the subjects. The Prussians of that day had the government which they deserved.

But reality, according to Hegel, is by no

FEUERBACH

means an attribute which belongs to a given social or political condition, under all circumstances and at all times. Quite the contrary. The Roman Republic was real, but the Roman Empire which replaced it was also real. The French Monarchy had become unreal in 1789, that is, it had lost all the quality of necessity, and was so contrary to reason that it had to be destroyed by the Great Revolution, of which Hegel always speaks with the greatest enthusiasm. Here, therefore, the monarchy was the unreal, the revolution the real. So in the course of progress all earlier reality becomes unreality, loses its necessity, its right of existence, its rationality; in place of the dying reality comes a new vital reality, peaceable when the old is sufficiently sensible to go to its death without a struggle, forcible when it strives against this necessity. And so the Hegelian statement through the Hegelian dialectic turns to its opposite—all that is real in the course of human history becomes in the process of time irrational and is, therefore, according to its destiny, irrational, and has from the beginning inherited want of

FEUERBACH

rationality, and everything which is reasonable in the minds of men is destined to become real, however much it may contradict the apparent reality of existing conditions. The statement of the rationality of everything real dissolves itself, according to the Hegelian mode of thought, in the other, "All that stands has ultimately only so much worth that it must fall."

But just there lay the true significance and the revolutionary character of the Hegelian philosophy (to which, as the conclusion of all progress since Kant, we must here limit ourselves) in that it, once and for all, gave the coup de grace to finiteness of results of human thought and action. Truth, which it is the province of philosophy to recognize, was no longer, according to Hegel, a collection of ready-made dogmatic statements, which once discovered must only be thoroughly learned; truth lay now in the process of knowledge itself, in the long historical development of learning, which climbs from lower to ever higher heights of knowledge, without ever reaching the point of so-called absolute truth, where it can go no further, where it has

FEUERBACH

nothing more to look forward to, except to fold its hands in its lap and contemplate the absolute truth already gained. And just as it is in the realm of philosophic knowledge, so is it with every other kind of knowledge, even with that of practical commerce. And just as little as knowledge can history find a conclusion, complete in one completed ideal condition of humanity, a completed society, a perfect state, are things which **can** only exist as phantasies, on the contrary, **all** successive historical conditions are **only** places of pilgrimage in the endless evolutionary progress of human society from the lower to the higher. Every step is necessary and useful for the time and circumstances to which it owes its origin, but it becomes weak and without justification under the newer and higher conditions which develop little by little in its own womb, it must give way to the higher form, which in turn comes to decay and defeat. As the bourgeoisie through the greater industry, competition, and the world market destroyed the practical value of all stable and anciently honored institutions, so this dialectic philosophy destroyed

FEUERBACH

all theories of absolute truth, and of an absolute state of humanity corresponding with them. In face of it nothing final, absolute or sacred exists, it assigns mortality indiscriminately, and nothing can exist before it save the unbroken process of coming into existence and passing away, the endless passing from the lower to the higher, the mere reflection of which in the brain of the thinker it is itself. It has indeed also a conservative side, it recognizes the suitability of a given condition of knowledge and society for its time and conditions, but only so far. This conservatism of this philosophical view is relative, its revolutionary character is absolute, the only absolute which it allows to exist.

We do not, at this point, need to go into the question whether this philosophy is consistent throughout with the present position of natural science which predicts for the earth a possible end and for its inhabitability, a fairly certain one; which, therefore, also recognizes that in human history there is not only an upshooting but also a down-growing branch. We find ourseles, at any rate, still a considerable distance

FEUERBACH

from the turning point, where the history of society begins to descend, and we cannot expect the Hegelian philosophy to meddle with a subject which at that time science had not yet placed upon the order of the day.

What must, indeed, be said is this, that the Hegelian development does not, according to Hegel, show itself so clearly. It is a necessary consequence of his method which he himself has never drawn with this explicitness. And for this simple reason, because he was compelled to make a system, and a system of philosophy must, in accordance with all its understood pretensions, close somewhere with a definition of absolute truth. So Hegel, therefore, in his logic, urged that this eternal truth is nothing else but the logical, that is, the historical process itself; yet in spite of this he finds himself compelled to place an end to this process, since he must come to an end with his system somewhere or other. He can make this end a beginning again in logic, since here the point of conclusion—the absolute idea, which is only absolute in so far as he has nothing clear to say about it—divests it-

FEUERBACH

self in nature, that is, becomes transformed, and later on, in spirit, that is, in thought and in history, comes to itself again. But in the last philosophical analysis, a return to the beginning is only possible in one way, namely, if one place the end of history in this fact, that mankind comes to a knowledge of the absolute idea, and explain that this knowledge of the absolute idea is obtained in the Hegelian philosophy. But in this way the whole dogmatic content of the Hegelian philosophy in the matter of absolute truth is explained in contradiction to his dialectic, the cutting loose from all dogmatic methods, and thereby the revolutionary side becomes smothered under the dominating conservative. And what can be said of philosophical knowledge can also be said of historical practice. Mankind, that is, in the person of Hegel, has arrived at the point of working out the absolute idea, and must also practically have arrived so far as to make the absolute idea a reality. The practical political demands of the abstract idea upon his contemporaries cannot, therefore, be stretched too far. And so we find as the conclusion of the philosophy

FEUERBACH

of Rights that the absolute idea shall realize itself in that limited monarchy which William III. so persistently, vainly promised to his subjects; therefore, in a limited, moderate, indirect control of the possessing classes, suitable to the dominating small bourgeois class in Germany whereby, in addition, the necessity to us of the existence of the nobility is shown in a speculative fashion.

The essential usefulness of the system is sufficient to explain the manufacture of a very tame political conclusion by means of a thoroughly revolutionary method of reasoning. The special form of this conclusion springs from this, as a matter of fact, that Hegel was a German, and, as in the case of his contemporary Goethe, he was somewhat of a philistine. Goethe and Hegel, each of them was an Olympian Zeus in his own sphere, but they were neither of them quite free from German philistinism.

But all this does not hinder the Hegelian system from playing an incomparably greater role than any earlier system and by virtue of this role developing riches of thought which are astounding even to-day.

FEUERBACH

Phemonology of the mind (which one may parallel with embryology and palaeontology of the mind), an evolution of the individual consciousness, through its different steps, expressed as a brief reproduction of the steps through which the consciousness of man has historically passed, logic, natural philosophy, mental philosophy, and the latter worked out separately in its detailed historical subdivisions, philosophy of history, of jurisprudence, of religion, history of philosophy, esthetics, etc. Hegel labored in all these different historical fields to discover and prove the thread of evolution, and as he was not only a creative genius, but also a man of encyclopedic learning, he was thus, from every point of view, the maker of an epoch. It is self-evident that by virtue of the necessities of the "System" he must very often take refuge in certain forced constructions, about which his pigmy opponents make such an ado even at the present time. But these constructions are only the frames and scaffoldings of his work; if one does not stop unnecessarily at these but presses on further into the building one will find uncounted

FEUERBACH

treasures which hold their full value to-day. As regards all philosophers, their system is doomed to perish and for this reason, because it emanates from an imperishable desire of the human soul, the desire to abolish all contradictions. But if all contradictions are once and for all disposed of, we have arrived at the so-called absolute truth, history is at an end, and yet it will continue to go on, although there is nothing further left for it to do—thus a newer and more insoluble contradiction. So soon as we have once perceived—and to this perception no one has helped us more than Hegel himself—that the task thus imposed upon philosophy signifies nothing different than the task that a single philosopher shall accomplish what it is only possible for the entire human race to accomplish, in the course of its progressive development—as soon as we understand that, it is all over with philosophy in the present sense of the word. In this way one discards the absolute truth, unattainable for the individual, and follows instead the relative truths attainable by way of the positive sciences, and the collection of their results by means of the dialectic mode

FEUERBACH

of thought. With Hegel universal philosophy comes to an end, on the one hand, because he comprehended in his system its entire development on the greatest possible scale; on the other hand, because he showed us the way, even if he did not know it himself, out of this labyrinth of systems, to a real positive knowledge of the world.

One may imagine what an immense effect the Hegelian philosophy produced in the philosophy-dyed atmosphere of Germany. The triumph lasted for ten years and by no means subsided with the death of Hegel. On the contrary, from 1830 to 1840 Hegelianism was exclusively supreme and had fastened itself upon its opponents to a greater or less degree. During this period Hegel's views, consciously or unconsciously, penetrated the different sciences, and saturated popular literature and the daily press from which the ordinary so-called cultured classes derive their mental pabulum. But this victory down the whole line was only preliminary to a conflict within its own ranks.

The entire doctrine of Hegel left, as we have seen, plenty of room for the bringing

FEUERBACH

under it the most diverse practical opinions, and the practical, in the then theoretic Germany, consisted in only two things — religion and politics. He who laid the greatest stress upon the Hegelian system, might be moderately conservative in both these respects, while he who considered the dialectic method of the greatest importance could belong to the extreme left in religious and political affairs. Hegel himself, in spite of the frequent outbursts of revolutionary wrath in his books, was inclined, on the whole, to the conservative side. His system, rather than his method, had cost him the hard thinking. At the end of the thirties, the division in the school grew greater and greater. The left wing, the so-called Young Hegelians, in their fight with the pious orthodox, abandoned little by little, that marked philosophical reserve regarding the burning questions of the day, which had up to that time secured for their teachings State toleration and even protection, and as in 1840 orthodox pietism and absolutist feudal reaction ascended the throne with Frederick William IV., open partisanship became unavoidable. The fight was still maintained

FEUERBACH

with philosophical weapons, but no longer along abstract philosophical lines; they went straight to deny the dominant religion and the existing state, and although in the "Deutschen Jahrbuechern" the practical aims were still put forward clothed in philosophical phraseology, the younger Hegelian school threw off disguise in the "Rheinische Zeitung," as the exponents of the philosophy of the struggling radicals, and used the cloak of philosophy only to deceive the censorship.

But politics were at that time a very thorny field, and so the main fight was directed against religion. But this was also, particularly since 1840, indirectly a political fight. Strauss' "Leben Jesu," published in 1835, had given the first cause of offense. The theory therein developed regarding the origin of the gospel myths Bruno Bauer later dealt with, adding the additional proof that a whole series of evangelical stories had been invented by their authors. The fight between these two was carried on under a philosophical disguise, as a battle of mind with matter; the question whether the marvellous stories

FEUERBACH

of the gospel came into being through an unconscious myth-creation in the womb of society, or whether they were individually invented by the evangelists broadened into the question whether in the history of the race, mind or matter carried the real weight, and lastly came Stirner, the prophet of modern anarchism—Bakunine has taken very much from him—and overtopped the sovereign power of consciousness with his sovereign power of the individual.

We do not follow the decomposition of the Hegelian school on this side any further. What is more important for us is this: The mass of the most decided young Hegelians were driven back upon English-French materialism through the necessities of their fight against positive religion. Here they came into conflict with their school system. According to materialism, nature exists as the sole reality, it exists in the Hegelian system only as the alienation of the absolute Idea, as it were a degradation of the Idea; under all circumstances, thought, and its thought-product, the Idea, according to this view, appears as the original, nature,

FEUERBACH

which only exists through the condescension of the Idea as the derived, and in this contradiction they got along as well or as ill as they might.

Then came Feuerbach's "Wesen des Christenthums." With one blow it cut the contradiction, in that it placed materialism on the throne again without any circumlocution. Nature exists independently of all philosophies. It is the foundation upon which we, ourselves products of nature, are built. Outside man and nature nothing exists, and the higher beings which our religious phantasies have created are only the fantastic reflections of our individuality. The cord was broken, the system was scattered and destroyed, the contradiction, since it only existed in the imagination, was solved. One must himself have experienced the delivering power of this book to get a clear idea of it. The enthusiasm was universal, we were all for the moment followers of Feuerbach. How enthusiastically Marx greeted the new idea and how much he was influenced by it, in spite of all his critical reservations, one may read in the "Holy Family."

FEUERBACH

The very faults of the book contributed to its momentary effect. The literary, impressive, even bombastic style secured for it a very large public and was a constant relief after the long years of abstract and abstruse Hegelianism. The same result also proceeded from the extravagant glorification of love, which in comparison with the insufferable sovereignty of pure reason, found an excuse, if not a justification. What we must not forget is, that just on these two weaknesses of Feuerbach "true Socialism" in educated Germany fastened itself like a spreading plague since 1844, and set literary phrases in the place of scientific knowledge, the freeing of mankind by means of love in place of the emancipation of the proletariat, through the economic transformation of production, in short lost itself in nauseous fine writing and in sickly sentimentality, of the type of which class of writers was Herr Karl Gruen.

We must furthermore not forget that though the Hegelian school was destroyed the Hegelian philosophy was not critically vanquished. Strauss and Bauer took each a side and engaged in polemics. Feuerbach

FEUERBACH

broke through the system and threw it as a whole aside. But one has not finished with a philosophy by simply declaring it to be false, and so enormous a work as the Hegelian philosophy which has had so tremendous an influence upon the mental development of the nation did not allow itself to be put aside peremptorily. It had to be destroyed in its own way, which means in the way that critically destroys its form but saves the new acquisitions to knowledge won by it. How this was brought about we shall see below.

But for the moment, the Revolution of 1848 put aside all philosophical discussion just as unceremoniously as Feuerbach laid aside Hegel. And then Feuerbach was himself crowded out.

FEUERBACH

II.

The great foundation question of all, especially new, philosophies is connected with the relation between thinking and being. Since very early times when men, being in complete ignorance respecting their own bodies, and stirred by apparitions,* arrived at the idea that thought and sensation were not acts of their own bodies, but of a special soul dwelling in the body and deserting it as death, ever since then they have been obliged to give thought to the relations of this soul to the outside world. If it betook itself from the body and lived on, there was no reason to invent another death for it; thus arose the conception of their immortality, which, at that evolutionary stage, did not appear as a consolation, but as fate, against which a man cannot strive, and often enough, as among the Greeks, as a positive misfortune. Not religious desire

---
*To this very day the idea is prevalent among savages and barbarians that the human forms appearing in our dreams are souls which temporarily leave the body, and that, therefore, the real man becomes liable for the deeds done to the dreamer by his dream appearance. So Imthurm, for example, found it in 1884 among the Indians in Guiana.

FEUERBACH

for consolation but uncertainty arising from a similar universal ignorance of what to associate with the soul when once it was acknowledged, after the death of the body, led universally to the tedious idea of personal immortality. Just in a similar fashion the first gods arose, through the personification of the forces of nature, and these in the further development of the religions acquired greater and greater supernatural force, until by a natural process of abstraction, I might say of distillation, from the many more or less limited and mutually limiting gods, in the course of spiritual development, at last the idea of the one all embracing god of the monotheistic religions took its place in the minds of men.

The question of the relation of thinking to being, of the relation of the spirit to nature, the highest question of universal philosophy, has therefore, no less than all religion, its roots in the limited and ignorant ideas of the condition of savagery. It could first be understood, and its full significance could first be grasped, when mankind awoke from the long winter sleep of Christian Middle Ages. The question of the

FEUERBACH

relation of thought to existence, a question which had also played a great role in the scholasticism of the Middle Ages, the question what is at the beginning spirit or nature, this question was in spite of the church now cut down to this: "Has God made the world or is the world from eternity?

As this question was answered this way or that the philosophers were divided into two great camps. The one party which placed the origin of the spirit before that of nature, and therefore in the last instance acepted creation, in some form or other—and this creation, is often according to the philosophers, according to Hegel for example, still more odd and impossible than in Christianity—made the camp of idealism. The others, who recognized nature as the source, belong to the various schools of materialism.

The two expressions signify something different from this. Idealism and materialism, originally not used in any other sense, are not here employed in any other sense. We shall see what confusion arises when one tries to force another signification into them.

FEUERBACH

The question of the relationship of thinking and being has another side; in what relation do our thoughts with regard to the world surrounding us stand to this world itself? Is our thought in a position to recognize the real world? Can we, in our ideas and notion of the real world, produce a correct reflection of the reality? This question is called in philosophical language the question of the identity of thinking and being, and is affirmed by the great majority of philosophers. According to Hegel, for example, its affirmation is self-evident, for that which we know in the actual world is its content, according to our thought, that which compels the world to a progressive realization as it were of the absolute Idea, which absolute idea has existed somewhere, unattached from the world and before the world; and that thought can recognize a content which is already a thought content herein, from the beginning, appears self-evident. It is also evident that what is here to be proved is already hidden in the hypothesis. But that does not hinder Hegel, by any means, from drawing the further conclusion from his proof of the identity of

FEUERBACH

thought and existence that his philosophy, because correct for his thought, is, therefore, the only correct one, and that the identity of thought and existence must show itself in this, that mankind should forthwith translate his philosophy from theory to practice and the whole world shift itself to a Hegelian base. This is an illusion which he shares alike with all philosophers.

In addition there is still another class of philosophers, those who dispute the possibility of a perception of the universe or at least of an exhaustive perception. To them belong, among the moderns, Hume and Kant, and they have played a very distinguished role in the evolution of philosophy. This point of view has been now refuted by Hegel, as far as possible, from the idealistic standpoint. The materialistic additions made by Feuerbach are more ingenious than deep. The most destructive refutation of this as of all other fixed philosophic ideas is actual result, namely experiment and industry. If we can prove the correctness of our idea of an actual occurrence by experiencing it ourselves and producing it from its constituent elements, and using it for our

FEUERBACH

own purposes into the bargain, the Kantian phrase "Ding an Sich" (thing in itself) ceases to have any meaning. The chemical substances which go to form the bodies of plants and animals remained just such "Dinge an Sich" until organic chemistry undertook to show them one after the other, whereupon the thing in itself became a thing for us, as the coloring matter in the roots of madder, alizarin, which we no longer allow to grow in the roots of the madder in the field, but make much more cheaply and simply from coal tar. The Copernican system was for three hundred years a hypothesis, with a hundred, a thousand, or ten thousand chances in its favor, but still a hypothesis. But when Leverrier by means of the data of this system not only discovered the existence of a certain unknown planet, but even calculated the position in the heavens which this planet must necessarily occupy, and when Galles really found this planet, then the Copernican system was proved. If, nevertheless, the resurrection of the Kantian idea in Germany is being tried by the Neo-Kantians, and of that of Hume in England (where they never died),

FEUERBACH

by the agnostics, that is, in the face of the long past theoretical and practical refutation of these doctrines, scientifically, a step backwards, and practically, merely the acceptance of materialism in a shame-faced way, clandestinely, and the denial of it before the world.

But the philosophers were during this long period from Descartes to Hegel and from Hobbes to Feuerbach by no means, as they thought, impelled solely by the force of pure reason. On the contrary, what really impelled them was, in particular, the strong and ever quicker conquering step of natural science and industry. Among the materialists this very quickly showed itself on the surface, but the idealistic systems filled themselves more and more with materialistic content and sought to reconcile the antagonism between spirit and matter by means of pantheism, so that finally the Hegelian system represented merely a materialism turned upside down, according to idealistic method and content.

Of course Starcke in his "Characteristics of Feuerbach" enquired into the fundamental question of the relations of thinking

FEUERBACH

and being. After a short introduction in which the ideas of preceding philosophers, particularly since Kant, are portrayed in unnecessarily heavy philosophical language and in which Hegel, owing to a too formal insistence on certain parts of his work does not receive due credit, there follows a copious description of the development of the metaphysics of Feuerbach, as shown in the course of the recognized writings of this philosopher. This description is industriously and carefully elaborated, and, like the whole book, is overballasted with, not always unavoidable, philosophical expressions, which is all the more annoying in that the writer does not hold to the vocabulary of one and the same school nor even of Feuerbach himself, but mixes up expressions of very different schools, and especially of the present epidemic of schools calling themselves philosophical.

The evolution of Feuerbach is that of a Hegelian to materialism—not of an orthodox Hegelian, indeed—an evolution which from a definite point makes a complete breach with the idealistic system of his predecessor. With irresistible force he brings

FEUERBACH

himself to the view that the Hegelian idea of the existence of the absolute idea before the world, the pre-existence of the logical categories before the universe came into being, is nothing else than the fantastical survival of the belief in the existence of an extramundane creator; that the material, sensible, actual world, to which we ourselves belong, is the only reality, and that our consciousness and thought, however supernatural they may seem, are only evidences of a material bodily organ, the brain. Matter is not a product of mind, but mind itself is only the highest product of matter. This is, of course, pure materialism. When he reached this point Feuerbach came to a standstill. He cannot overcome ordinary philosophical prejudice, prejudice not against the thing, but against the name materialism. He says "Materialism is for me the foundation of the building of the being and knowledge of man, but it is not for me what it is for the physiologists in the narrow sense, as Moleschott, for example, since necessarily from their standpoint it is the building itself. Backwards, I am in accord with the materialists but not forwards."

FEUERBACH

Feuerbach here confuses materialism, which is a philosophy of the universe dependent upon a certain comprehension of the relations between matter and spirit, with the special forms in which this philosophy appeared at a certain historical stage—namely in the eighteenth century. More than that he confuses it with the shallow and vulgarized form in which the materialism of the eighteenth century exists today, in the minds of naturalists and physicians, and was popularized during a period of fifty years in the writings of Buechner, Vogt and Moleschott. But as idealism has passed through a series of evolutionary developments, so also has materialism—with each epoch-making discovery in the department of natural science it has been obliged to change its form; since then, history also, being subjected to the materialistic method of treatment, shows itself as a new road of progress.

The materialism of the preceding century was overwhelmingly mechanical, because at that time of all the natural sciences, mechanics, and indeed, only the mechanics of the celestial and terrestrial fixed bodies, the

FEUERBACH

mechanics of gravity, in short, had reached any definite conclusions. Chemistry existed at first only in a childish, phlogistic form. Biology still lay in swaddling clothes; the organism of plants and animals was examined only in a very cursory manner, and was explained upon purely mechanical grounds; just as an animal was to Descartes nothing but a machine, so was man to the materialists of the eighteenth century. The exclusive application of the measure of mechanics to processes which are of chemical and organic nature and by which, it is true, the laws of mechanics are also manifested, but are pushed into the background by other higher laws, this application is the cause of the peculiar, but, considering the times, unavoidable, narrowmindedness of the French materialism.

The second special limitation of this materialism lies in its incapacity to represent the universe as a process, as one form of matter assumed in the course of evolutionary development. This limitation corresponded with the natural science of the time and the metaphysic coincident therewith, that is the anti-dialectic methods of the phil-

FEUERBACH

osophers. Nature, as was known, was in constant motion, but this motion, according to the universally accepted ideas, turned eternally in a circle, and therefore never moved from the spot, and produced the same results over and over again. This idea was at that time inevitable. The Kantian theory of the origin of the solar system was at first exhibited and considered as a mere curiosity. The history of the development of the earth-geology was still unknown, and the idea that the living natural objects of to-day are the result of a long process of development from the simple to the complex could not be scientifically established at that time. This anti-historical comprehension of nature was, therefore, inevitable. We cannot reproach the philosophers of the eighteenth century with this, as the same thing is also found in Hegel. According to him, nature is the mere outward form of the Idea, capable of no progress as regards time, but merely of an extension of its manifoldness in space, so that it displays all the stages of development comprised in it at one and the same time together, and is condemned to a repetition of the same processes. And this

FEUERBACH

absurdity of a progress in space but outside of time—the fundamental condition of all progress—Hegel loads upon nature, just at the very time when geology, embryology, the physiology of plants and animals, and inorganic chemistry, were being built up, and when above all genial prophecies of the later evolution theory appeared at the very threshold of these new sciences (e. g., Goethe and Lamark), but the system so required it, and the method, for love of the system, had to prove untrue to itself.

This unhistoric conception had its effects also in the domain of history. Here the fight against the remnants of the Middle Ages kept the outlook limited. The Middle Ages were reckoned as a mere interruption of history by a thousand years of barbarism. The great advances of the Middle Ages—the broadening of European learning, the bringing into existence of great nations, which arose, one after the other, and finally the enormous technical advances of the fourteenth and fifteenth centuries—all this no one saw. Consequently a rational view of the great historic development was rendered impossible, and history served prin-

FEUERBACH

cipally as a collection of examples and illustrations for the use of philosophers.

The vulgarizing peddlers who during the fifties occupied themselves with materialism in Germany did not by any means escape the limitations of their doctrine. All the advances made in science served them only as new grounds of proof against the existence of the Creator, and indeed it was far beyond their trade to develop the theory any further. Idealism was at the end of its tether and was smitten with death by the Revolution of 1848. Yet it had the satisfaction that materialism sank still lower. Feuerbach was decidedly right when he refused to take the responsibility of this materialism, only he had no business to confound the teachings of the itinerant spouters with materialism in general.

However, we must here remark two different things. During the life of Feuerbach science was still in that state of violent fermentation which has only comparatively cleared during the last fifteen years; new material of knowledge was furnished in a hitherto unheard of measure but the fixing of interrelations, and therewith of order, in

FEUERBACH

the chaos of overwhelming discoveries was rendered possible quite lately for the first time. True, Feuerbach had lived to see the three distinctive discoveries — that of the cell, the transformation of energy and the evolution theory acknowledged since the time of Darwin. But how could the solitary country-dwelling philosopher appreciate at their full value discoveries which naturalists themselves at that time in part contested and partly did not understand how to avail themselves of sufficiently? The disgrace falls solely upon the miserable conditions in Germany owing to which the chairs of philosophy were filled by pettifogging eclectic pedants, while Feuerbach, who towered high above them all, had to rusticate and grow sour in a little village. It is therefore no shame to Feuerbach that he never grasped the natural evolutionary philosophy which became possible with the passing away of the partial views of French materialism.

In the second place, Feuerbach held quite correctly that scientific materialism is the foundation of the building of human knowledge but it is not the building itself. For

FEUERBACH

we live not only in nature but in human society, and this has its theory of development and its science no less than nature. It was necessary, therefore, to bring the science of society, that is the so-called historical and philosophical sciences, into harmony with the materialistic foundations and to rebuild upon them. But this was not granted to Feuerbach. Here he stuck, in spite of the "foundations," held in the confining bonds of idealism, and to this he testified in the words "Backwards I am with the materialists, but not forwards." But Feuerbach himself did not go forward in his views of human society from his standpoint of 1840 and 1844, chiefly owing to that loneliness which compelled him to think everything out by himself, instead of in friendly and hostile conflict with other men of his calibre, although of all philosophers he was the fondest of intercourse with his fellows. We shall see later on how he thus remained an idealist. Here we can only call attention to the fact that Starcke sought the idealism of Feuerbach in the wrong place. "Feuerbach is an idealist; he believes in the advance of mankind" (p.

FEUERBACH

19). " The foundations, the underpinning of the whole, is therefore nothing less than idealism. Realism is for us nothing more than a protection against error while we follow our own idealistic tendencies. Are not compassion, love and enthusiasm for truth and justice ideal forces?"

In the first place, idealism is here defined as nothing but the following of ideal aims. But these have necessarily to do principally with the idealism of Kant and his "Categorical Imperative." But Kant himself called his philosophy "transcendental idealism," by no means, because he deals therein with moral ideals, but on quite other grounds, as Starcke will remember.

The superstition that philosophical idealism pivots around a belief in moral, that is in social ideals, arose with the German non-philosophical Philistine, who commits to memory the few philosophical morsels which he finds in Schiller's poems. Nobody has criticised more severely the feeble Categorical Imperative of Kant—feeble because it demands the impossible and therefore never attains to any reality—nobody has ridiculed more cruelly the Philistine

FEUERBACH

sentimentality imparted by Schiller, because of its unrealizable ideals, than just the idealist par excellence, Hegel. (See e. g. Phenomonology.)

In the second place, it cannot be avoided that all human sensations pass through the brain—even eating and drinking which are commenced consequent upon hunger and thirst felt by the brain and ended in consequence of sensations of satisfaction similarly experienced by the brain. The realities of the outer world impress themselves upon the brain of man, reflect themselves there, as feelings, thoughts, impulses, volitions, in short, as ideal tendencies, and in this form become ideal forces. If the circumstance that this man follows ideal tendencies at all, and admits that ideal forces exercise an influence over him, if this makes an idealist of him, every normally developed man is in some sense a born idealist, and under such circumstances how can materialists exist?

In the third place, the conviction that humanity, at least at present, as a whole, progresses, has absolutely nothing to do with the antagonism between materialism and

FEUERBACH

idealism. The French materialists had this conviction, to a fanatical degree, no less than the deists, Voltaire and Rousseau, and made the greatest personal sacrifices for it. If anybody ever concentrated his whole life to the enthusiasm for truth and justice, taking the words in a moral sense, it was Diderot, for example. Therefore, since Starcke has explained all this as idealism, it simply proves that the word materialism has lost all significance for him, as has also the antagonism between the aims of the two.

The fact is that Starcke here makes an unpardonable concession to the prejudices of the Philistines caused by the long continued slanders of the clergy against the word materialism, even if without consciously doing so. The Philistine understands by the word materialism, gluttony, drunkenness, carnal lust, and fraudulent speculation, in short all the enormous vices to which he himself is secretly addicted, and by the word idealism he understands the belief in virtue, universal humanitarianism, and a better world as a whole, of which he boasts before others, and in which he himself at the very most believes, only as long as he must endure

FEUERBACH

the blues which follow necessarily from his customary "materialistic" excesses, and so sings his favorite song—"What is man?—Half beast, half angel."

As for the rest, Starcke takes great pains to defend Feuerbach against the attacks and doctrines of those collegians who plume themselves in Germany as philosophers now-a-days. It is true that this is a matter of importance to those people who take an interest in the afterbirth of the German classic philosophy, to Starcke himself this might appear necessary. We spare the reader this, however.

FEUERBACH

III.

The distinct idealism of Feuerbach is evident directly we come to his philosophy of religion and ethics. He does not wish to abolish religion by any means; he wants to perfect it. Philosophy itself will be absorbed in religion. "The periods of human progress are only distinguishable by religious changes. There is only a real historical progress where it enters the hearts of men. The heart is not a place for religion, so that it should be in the heart, it is the very being of religion." Religion is, according to Feuerbach, a matter of the feelings—the feelings of love between man and man which up to now sought its realization in the fantastic reflected image of the reality—in the interposition through one or more gods of the fantastic reflections of human qualities—but now by means of love between "ego" and "tu" finds itself directly and without any intermediary. According to Feuerbach love between the sexes is, if not the highest form, at least one of the highest forms, of the practice of his new religion.

FEUERBACH

Now, feelings of affection between man and man, and particularly between members of the two sexes, have existed as long as mankind has. Love between the sexes has been cultivated especially during the last eighteen hundred years and has won a place which has made it, in this period, a compulsory motive for all poetry. The existing positive religions have limited themselves in this matter to the bestowal of complete consecration upon the State regulation of sexual love, and might completely disappear tomorrow without the least difference taking place in the matter of love and friendship. Thus the Christian religion in France was, as a matter of fact, so completely overthrown between the years 1793 and 1798, that Napoleon himself could not re-introduce it without opposition and difficulty, without, in the interval, any desire for a substitute, in Feuerbach's sense, making itself felt.

Feuerbach's idealism consists in this, that he does not simply take for granted the mutual and reciprocal feelings of men for one another such as sexual love, friendship, compassion, self-sacrifice, etc., but declares that

FEUERBACH

they would come to their full realization for the first time as soon as they were consecrated under the name of religion. The main fact for him is not that these purely human relations exist, but that they will be conceived of as the new true religion. They will be fully realized for the first time if they are stamped as religions. Religion is derived from "religare" and means originally "fastening." Therefore, every bond between men is religion. Such etymological artifices are the last resort of the idealistic philosophy. Not what the word means according to the historical development of its true significance, but what it should mean according to its derivation is what counts, and so sex-love and the intercourse between the sexes is consecrated as a "religion" only so that the word religion, which is dear to the mind of the idealist, shall not vanish from the language. The Parisian reformer of the stripe of Louis Blanc used to speak just in the same way in the forties, for they could only conceive of a man without religion as a monster, and used to say to us "Atheism, then, is your religion."

If Feuerbach wants to place true religion

FEUERBACH

upon the basis of real materialistic philosophy, that would be just the same as conceiving of modern chemistry as true alchemy. If religion can exist without its God then alchemy can exist without its philosopher's stone. There exists, by the way, a very close connection between alchemy and religion. The philosopher's stone has many properties of the old gods, and the Egyptian-Greek alchemists of the first two centuries of our era have had their hands in the development of Christian doctrines, as Kopp and Berthelot prove.

Feuerbach's declaration that the periods of man's development are only differentiated through changes in religion is false. Great historical points of departure are coincident with religious changes only as far as the three world-religions which exist up to the present are concerned—Buddhism, Christianity and Islam. The old tribal and national religions originating in nature were not propagandist and lost all power of resistance as soon as the independence of the tribe and people was destroyed. Among the Germans simple contact with the decaying Roman Empire and the Christian world-

FEUERBACH

religion springing from it and suitable to its economic, political and ideal circumstances, was sufficient. In the first place, as regards these more or less artificial world-religions, particularly in the cases of Christianity and Mohammedanism, we find that the more universal historical movements will take on a religious stamp, and as far as concerns Christianity in particular, the stamp of the religion affecting revolutionary movements of universal significance stopped short at the commencement of the fight of the bourgeois for emancipation from the thirteenth to the seventeenth century, and showed itself not as Feuerbach declares in the hearts of men and the thirst for religion, but in the entire earlier history of the Middle Ages which knew no other form of idealism than religion and theology. But as the bourgeoisie in the eighteenth century was sufficiently strong to have its own ideology suitable to its own standpoint, it forthwith made its great and final revolution, the French, by means of an appeal exclusively to juristic and political ideals, and troubled itself with religion only so far as it stood in its way. It never occurred to it

FEUERBACH

to establish a new religion in place of the old one; everybody knows what a mess Robespierre made of the attempt.

The possibility of a purely humane sentiment in intercourse with other men is with us today exceedingly impeded through the society founded on class antagonism and class supremacy in which we must move. We have no need to trouble ourselves about sanctifying these sentiments by means of a new religion. And just as the circumstances of the great historical class-fight have been obscured by the current historians, particularly in Germany, so in the same way the understanding of the great historical class-conflicts is sufficiently obscured by the present-day manner of writing history, without our needing to change these conflicts into a mere appendix of ecclesiastical history. Here it is evident how far we in our day are away from Feuerbach. His most beautiful passages in praise of the new religion of love are today unreadable.

The only religion which Feuerbach examined closely is Christianity, the universal religion of the western world which is founded upon monotheism. He proves that

FEUERBACH

the Christian God is only the fantastic reflection, the reflected image of man. But that God is himself the product of a lengthy process of abstraction, the concentrated quintessence of the earlier tribal and national gods. And man also whose reflection that God is, is not a real man, but is likewise the quintessence of many real men, the abstract human, and therefore himself again the creature of thought. The same Feuerbach who on each page preaches sensation, diving into the concrete, the real, becomes thoroughly abstract as soon as he begins to talk of more than mere sensual intercourse between human beings.

Of this relationship only one side appeals to him, the moral, and Feuerbach's astonishing lack of resources as compared with Hegel is striking. The ethic or rather moral doctrine of the latter, is the Philosophy of Right and embraces: 1, Abstract Right; 2, Morality; 3, Moral Conduct, under which are again comprised: the family, bourgeois, society, and the State. As the form is here idealistic, the content is realistic. The entire scope of law, economy, politics, is therein, besides ethics. With Feuerbach, it is just

FEUERBACH

the reverse. He is realistic in form; he begins with man, but the discussion has absolutely nothing to do with the world in which this man lives, and so, instead of the man, stands an abstract man, who preaches sermons concerning the philosophy of religion. This man is not even the son of a mother; he has developed from the God of the monotheistic religions. He does not live in real historic conditions and the world of history. He comes into relationship with other men, but each of the others is just as much an abstraction as he himself is. In the "philosophy of religion" we had still men and women, but in the "ethic" this final distinction vanishes. At long intervals Feuerbach makes such statements as: "A man thinks differently in a palace than in a hut." "When you have nothing in your body to ward off hunger and misery, you have nothing in your head, mind and heart for morality." "Politics must be our religion," etc. But Feuerbach was absolutely incapable of extracting any meaning from these remarks; they remain purely literary expressions, and Starcke himself is obliged to admit that the science of politics was an insuperable obstacle to

FEUERBACH

Feuerbach and the science of society, sociology, for him a terra incognita.

He appears just as uninspired in comparison with Hegel in his treatment of the antithesis of good and evil. "One thinks he is saying something great," Hegel remarks "if one says that mankind is by nature good, but it is forgotten that one says something far greater in the words "man is by nature evil." According to Hegel, evil is the form in which the mechanical power of evolution shows itself, and indeed in this lies the double idea that each new step forward appears as an outrage against a sacred thing, as rebellion against the old, dying, but through custom, sanctified, circumstances, and on the other hand that since the rising of class antagonism, the evil passions of men, greed and imperiousness serve as the levers of historical progress, of which, for example, the history of feudalism and the bourgeoisie affords a conspicuous proof. But Feuerbach does not trouble himself to examine the role of moral evil. History is to him a particularly barren and unwonted field. Even his statement, "Man as he sprang from nature originally was

FEUERBACH

only a mere creature, not a man." "Man is a product of human society, of education, and of history." Even this statement remains from his standpoint absolutely unproductive.

What Feuerbach communicates to us respecting morals must therefore be exceedingly narrow. The desire for happiness is born within man and must hence be the foundation of all morality. But the desire for happiness is limited in two ways; first, through the natural results of our acts; after the dissipation comes the headache, as a result of habitual excess, sickness; in the second place, through its results upon society, if we do not respect the similar desire for happiness on the part of other people, they resist us and spoil our pursuit of happiness. It follows, therefore, that in order to enjoy our pursuit of happiness, the result of our acts must be rightly appreciated, and, on the other hand, must allow of the carrying out of the same acts on the part of others. Practical self-control with regard to ourselves and love, always love, in our intercourse with others are therefore the foundation rules of Feuerbach's morality,

FEUERBACH

from which all others lead, and neither the enthusiastic periods of Feuerbach nor the loud praises of Starcke can set off the thinness and flatness of this pair of utterances.

The desire for happiness contents itself only very exceptionally, and by no means to the profit of one's self or other people with self. But it requires the outside world—means of satisfying itself—therefore means of subsistence, an individual of the other sex, books, convention, argument, activity, these means and matters of satisfaction are matters of utility and labor. Feuerbach's system of morality either predicates that these means and matters of satisfaction are given to every man *per se,* or, since it gives him only unpractical advice, is not worth a jot to the people who are without these means. And this Feuerbach himself shows clearly in forcible words, "One thinks differently in a palace than in a hut." "Where owing to misery and hunger you have no material in your body, you have also no material in your head, mind and heart for morals.

Are matters any better with the equal right of another to the pursut of happiness?

FEUERBACH

Feuerbach set this statement out as absolute, as applicable to all times and circumstances. But since when has it been true? Was there in the olden time between slave and master or in the Middle Ages between serf and baron any talk about equal rights to the pursuit of happiness? Was not the right to the pursuit of happiness of the subject class sacrificed to the dominant class regardlessly and by means of law?—nay, that was immoral, but still equality of rights is recognized now-a-days—recognized in words merely since the bourgeoisie in its fight against feudalism and in the institution of capitalistic production, was compelled to abolish all existing exclusive, that is, personal, privileges, and for the first time to introduce the right of the private individual, then also gradually the right of the State, and equality before law. But the pursuit of happiness consists for the least part only in ideal rights, and lies, for the most part, in means of material satisfaction takes care that only enough for bare subsistence falls to the great majority of those persons with equal rights, and there-

FEUERBACH

fore regards the equality of right to the pursuit of happiness hardly better than slavery or serfdom did. And are we better off as regards mental means of happiness—means of education? Is not the schoolmaster of Sadowa a mythical person?

Further, according to the ethical theory of Feuerbach, the Bourse is the highest temple of morality, only provided that one speculate rightly. If my pursuit of happiness leads me to the Bourse, and I, in following my business, manage so well that only what is agreeable and nothing detrimental comes to me, that is that I win steadily, Feuerbach's precept is carried out. In this way I do not interfere with the similar pursuit of happiness of anyone else, since the other man goes on the Bourse just as voluntarily as I do, and at the conclusion of his affairs a sentimental expression, for each finds in the other the satisfaction of his pursuit of happiness which it is just the business of love to bring about, and which it here practically accomplishes. And since I carry on my operations with more exact prudence and therefore with greater success I fulfill the strongest maxims of the Feuerbach mor-

FEUERBACH

al philosophy and become a rich man into the bargain. In other words, Feuerbach's morality is hewn out of the capitalistic system of today, little as he might wish or think it to be.

But love, yes love, is particularly and eternally the magical god who, according to Feuerbach, surmounts all the difficulties of practical life and that in a society which is divided into classes with diametrically opposing interests. The last remnant of its revolutionary character is thus taken from his philosophy, and there remains the old cant—"love one another"—fall into each other's arms without regard to any impediment of sex or position—universal intoxication of reconciliation.

In a word, the moral theories of Feuerbach turn out to be the same as those of all of his predecessors. It is a hodge-podge of all times, all people, and all conditions, and for this occasion is applicable to no time and place, and as regards the actual world is as powerless as Kant's "Categorical Imperative." As a matter of fact, every class, as well as every profession, has its own system of morals and breaks even this when it

FEUERBACH

can do it without punishment, and love, which is to unite all, appears today in wars, controversies, lawsuits, domestic broils and as far as possible mutual plunder.

But how was it possible that the powerful impetus given by Feuerbach turned out so unprofitable to Feuerbach himself. Simply in this way, because Feuerbach could not find his way out of the abstraction, which he hated with a deadly hatred, to living reality. He clutches hard at Nature and Humanity, but "Nature" and "Humanity" remain empty words with him. He does not know how to tell us anything positive about real nature and real men. We can only reach living men from the abstract men of Feuerbach if we regard them as active historical agents. Feuerbach strove against that, hence the year 1848, which he did not understand, signified for him merely the final break with the real world, retirement into solitude. German conditions must for the most part bear the guilt of allowing him to starve miserably.

But the step which Feuerbach did not make had not yet been made. The cultus of man in the abstract which was the kernel of

FEUERBACH

Feuerbach's religion must be replaced by the knowledge of real men and their historical development. This advance of Feuerbach's view beyond Feuerbach himself was published in 1845 by Marx in the "Holy Family."

FEUERBACH

IV.

Strauss, Bauer, Stirner, Feuerbach, these were the minor representatives of the Hegelian philosophy, so far as they did not abandon the field of philosophy. Strauss has, in addition to the "Life of Jesus" and "Dogmatics," only produced philosophical and ecclesiastical historical work of a literary character, after the fashion of Renan; Bauer has merely done something in the department of primitive Christianity, but that significant; Stirner remained a "freak" even after Bakunine had mixed him with Proudhon and designated his amalgamation "Anarchism." Feuerbach alone possessed any significance as a philosopher; but not only did philosophy remain for him the vaunted superior of all other sciences, the quintessence of all science, an impassable limitation, the untouchable holy thing, he stood as a composite philosopher; the under half of him was materialist, the upper half idealist. He was not an apt critic of Hegel

FEUERBACH

but simply put him aside as of no account, while he himself, in comparison with the encyclopedic wealth of the Hegelian system, contributed nothing of any positive value, except a bombastic religion of love and a thin, impotent system of ethics.

But from the breaking up of the Hegelian school there proceeded another, the only one which has borne real fruit, and this tendency is coupled with the name of Marx.*

In this case the separation from the Hegelian philosophy occurred by means of a return to the materialistic standpoint, that is to say, a determination to comprehend the actual world — nature and history — as it presents itself to each one of us, without any

---

*It is incumbent upon me to make a personal explanation at this place. People have lately referred to my share in this theory, and so I can hardly refrain from saying a few words here in settlement of that particular matter. I cannot deny that I had before and during my forty years' collaboration with Marx a certain independent share not only in laying out the foundations, but more particularly in working out the theory. But the greatest part of the leading essential thinking, particularly in the realm of economics, and especially its final sharp statement, belongs to Marx alone. What I contributed Marx could quite readily have carried out without me with the exception of a pair of special applications. What Marx supplied, I could not have readily brought. Marx stood higher, saw further, took a wider, clearer, quicker survey than all of us. Marx was a genius, we others, at the best, talented. Without him the theory would not be what it is today, by a long way. It therefore rightly bears his name.

FEUERBACH

preconceived idealistic balderdash interfering; it was resolved to pitilessly sacrifice any idealistic preconceived notion which could not be brought into harmony with facts actually discovered in their mutual relations, and without any visionary notions. And materialism in general claims no more. Only here, for the first time in the history of the materialistic philosophy, was an earnest endeavor made to carry its results to all questions arising in the realm of knowledge, at least in its characteristic features.

Hegel was not merely put on one side, the school attached itself on the contrary to his openly revolutionary side, the dialectic method. But this method was of no service in its Hegelian form. According to Hegel the dialectic is the self-development of the Idea. The Absolute Idea does not only exist from eternity, but it is also the actual living soul of the whole existing world. It develops from itself to itself through all the preliminary stages which are treated of at large in "Logic," and which are all included in it. Then it steps outside of itself, changing with nature itself, where it, with-

FEUERBACH

out self-consciousness, is disguised as a necessity of nature, goes through a new development, and, finally, in man himself, becomes self-consciousness. This self-consciousness now works itself out into the higher stages from the lower forms of matter, until finally the Absolute Idea is again realized in the Hegelian philosophy. According to Hegel, the dialectic development apparent in nature and history, that is a causative, connected progression from the lower to the higher, in spite of all zig-zag movements and momentary setbacks, is only the stereotype of the self-progression of the Idea from eternity, whither one does not know, but independent at all events of the thought of any human brain. This topsy-turvy ideology had to be put aside. We conceived of ideas as materialistic, as pictures of real things, instead of real things as pictures of this or that stage of the Absolute Idea. Thereupon, the dialectic became reduced to knowledge of the universal laws of motion—as well of the outer world as of the thought of man—two sets of laws which are identical as far as matter is concerned but which differ as re-

FEUERBACH

gards expression, in so far as the mind of man can employ them consciously, while, in nature, and up to now, in human history, for the most part they accomplish themselves, unconsciously in the form of external necessity, through an endless succession of apparent accidents. Hereupon the dialectic of the Idea became itself merely the conscious reflex of the dialectic evolution of the real world, and therefore, the dialectic of Hegel was turned upside down or rather it was placed upon its feet instead of on its head, where it was standing before. And this materialistic dialectic which since that time has been our best tool and our sharpest weapon was discovered, not by us alone, but by a German workman, Joseph Dietzgen, in a remarkable manner and utterly independent of us.

But just here the revolutionary side of Hegel's philosophy was again taken up, and at the same time freed from the idealistic frippery which had in Hegel's hands interfered with its necessary conclusions. The great fundamental thought, namely, that the world is not to be considered as a complexity of ready-made things, but as a com-

FEUERBACH

plexity made up of processes in which the apparently stable things, no less than the thought pictures in the brain—the idea, cause an unbroken chain of coming into being and passing away, in which, by means of all sorts of seeming accidents, and in spite of all momentary setbacks, there is carried out in the end a progressive development—this great foundation thought has, particularly since the time of Hegel, so dominated the thoughts of the mass of men that, generally speaking, it is now hardly denied. But to acknowledge it in phrases, and to apply it in reality to each particular set of conditions which come up for examination, are two different matters. But if one proceeds steadily in his investigations from this historic point, then a stop is put, once and for all, to the demand for final solutions and for eternal truths; one is firmly conscious of the necessary limitations of all acquired knowledge, of its hypothetical nature, owing to the circumstances under which it has been gained. One cannot be imposed upon any longer by the inflated insubstantial antitheses of the older metaphysics of true and

FEUERBACH

false, good and evil, identical and differentiated, necessary and accidental; one knows that these antitheses have only a relative significance, that that which is recognized as true now, has its concealed and later-developing false side, just as that which is recognized as false, its true side, by virtue of which it can later on prevail as the truth; that so-called necessity is made up of the merely accidental, and that the acknowledged accidental is the form behind which necessity conceals itself and so on.

The old methods of enquiry and thought which Hegel terms metaphysics, which by preference busied themselves by enquiring into things as given and established quantities, and the vestiges of which still buzz in the heads of people, had at that time great historical justification. Things had first to be examined, before it was possible to examine processes; man must first know what a thing was before he could examine the preceding changes in it. And so it was with natural science. The old metaphysic which comprehended things as stable came from a philosophy which enquired into dead and living things as things comprehended as stable.

FEUERBACH

But when this enquiry had so far progressed that the decisive step was possible, namely, the systematic examination of the preceding changes in those things going on in nature itself, then occurred the death-blow of the old metaphysics in the realm of philosophy. And, in fact, if science to the end of the last century was chiefly a collecting of knowledge, the science of actual things, so is science in our day pre-eminently an arranging of knowledge, the science of changes, of the origin and progress of things, and the mutual connection which binds these changes in nature into one great whole. Physiology, which examines the earlier forms of plant and animal organisms; embryology, which deals with the development of the elementary organism from germ to maturity; geology, which investigates the gradual formation of the earth's crust, are all the products of our century.

But, first of all, there are three great discoveries which have caused our knowledge of the interdependence of the processes of nature to progress by leaps and bounds. In the first place, the discovery of the cell, as the unit, from the multiplication and differ-

FEUERBACH

entiation of which, the whole of plant and animal substance develop so that not only the growth and development of all higher classes of all higher organisms is recognized as following a universal law, but the very path is shown in the capacity for differentiation in the cell, by which organisms are enabled to change their forms and make thereby a more individual development. Secondly, the metamorphosis of energy which has shown us that all the so-called real forces in inorganic nature, the mechanical forces and their complements, the so-called potential energies, heat, radiation (light, radiating heat), electricity, magnetism, chemical energy, are different forms of universal motion, which pass, under certain conditions, the one into the other, so that in place of those of the one which disappear, a certain number of the other appear, so that the whole movement of nature is reduced to this perpetual process of transformation from one into the other. Finally, the proof first developed logically by Darwin, that the organic products of nature about us, including man, are the result of a long process of evolution,

FEUERBACH

from a few original single cells, and these again, by virtue of chemical processes, have proceeded from protoplasm or white of egg.

Thanks to these three great discoveries and the resultant powerful advance of science, we have now arrived at a point where we can show the connection between changes in nature, not only in specific cases, but also in the relation of the specific cases to the whole and so give a bird's eye view of the interrelation of nature in an approximately scientific form by means of the facts shown by empirical science itself. To furnish this complete picture was formerly the task of the so-called philosophy of nature. It could then only do this by substituting ideal and imaginary hypotheses for the unknown real interconnection, by filling out the missing facts with mind-pictures and by bridging the chasms by empty imaginings. It had many happy thoughts in these transports (of imagination), it anticipated many later discoveries, but it also caused the survival of considerable nonsense up to the present time which could not otherwise have been possible. At present, when the results of the investigation of nature need only be con-

FEUERBACH

conceived of dialectically, that is in the sense of their mutual interconnection, to arrive at a system of nature sufficient for our time, when the dialectical character of this interconnection forces itself into the metaphysically trained minds of experimental scientists, against their will, today a philosophy of nature is finally disposed of, every attempt at its resurrection would not only be superfluous, it would even be a step backwards.

But what is true of nature, which is hereby recognized as an historical process, is true also of the history of society in all its branches, and of the totality of all sciences which occupy themselves with things human and divine. Here also the philosophy of jurisprudence, of history, of religion, etc., consisted in this, that in place of the true interconnection of events, one originating in the mind of the philosopher was substituted; that history, in its totality as in its parts, was comprehended as the gradual realization of ideas, but, of course, always of the pet idea of the philosopher himself.

History worked up to now, unconsciously but necessarily, towards a certain prede-

FEUERBACH

termined, fixed, ideal goal, as for example in the case of Hegel, towards the realization of his Absolute Idea, and the unalterable trend towards this Absolute Idea constituted the inward connection of historic facts. In the place of the real, and up to this time unknown, interrelation, man set a new mysterious destiny, unconscious or gradually coming into consciousness. It was necessary in this case, therefore, just as in the realm of nature, to set aside these artificial interrelations by the discovery of the real, a task which finally culminated in the discovery of the universal laws of progress, which established themselves as the dominating ones in the history of human society.

The history of the growth of society appears, however, in one respect entirely different from that of nature. In nature are to be found as far as we leave the reaction of man upon nature out of sight—mere unconscious blind agents which act one upon another, and in their interplay the universal law realizes itself. From all that happens, whether from the innumerable apparent accidents which appear upon the surface, or from the final results flowing from these accidental

FEUERBACH

occurrences, nothing occurs as a desired conscious end. On the contrary, in the history of society the mere actors are all endowed with consciousness; they are agents imbued with deliberation or passion, men working towards an appointed end; nothing appears without an intentional purpose, without an end desired. But this distinction, important as it is for historical examination, particularly of single epochs and events, can make no difference to the fact that the course of history is governed by inner universal laws. Here also, in spite of the wished for aims of all the separate individuals, accident for the most part is apparent on the surface. That which is willed but rarely happens. In the majority of instances the numerous desired ends cross and interfere with each other, and either these ends are utterly incapable of realization, or the means are ineffectual. So, the innumerable conflicts of individual wills and individual agents in the realm of history reach a conclusion which is on the whole analogous to that in the realm of nature, which is without definite purpose. The ends of the actions are intended, but the re-

FEUERBACH

sults which follow from the actions are not intended, or in so far as they appear to correspond with the end desired, in their final results are quite different from the conclusion wished. Historical events in their entirety therefore appear to be likewise controlled by chance. But even where according to superficial observation, accident plays a part, it is, as a matter of fact, consistently governed by unseen, internal laws, and the only qestion remaining, therefore, is to discover these laws.

Men make their own history in that each follows his own desired ends independent of results, and the results of these many wills acting in different directions and their manifold effects upon the world constitute history. It depends, therefore, upon what the great majority of individuals intend. The will is determined by passion or reflection, but the levers which passion or reflection immediately apply are of very different kinds. Sometimes it may be external circumstances, sometimes ideal motives, zeal for honor, enthusiasm for truth and justice, personal hate, or even purely individual peculiar ideas of all kinds. But on the one

FEUERBACH

hand, we have seen in history that the results of many individual wills produce effects, for the most part quite other than what is wished—often, in fact, the very opposite—their motives of action, likewise, are only of subordinate significance with regard to the universal result. On the other hand, the question arises: What driving forces stand in turn behind these motives of action; what are the historical causes which transform themselves into motives of action in the brains of the agents?

The old materialism never set this question before itself. Its philosophy of history, as far as it ever had one in particular, is hence essentially pragmatic; it judges everything from the standpoint of the immediate motive; it divides historical agents into good and bad and finds as a whole that the good are defrauded and the bad are victorious, whence it follows that, as far as the old materialism is concerned, there is nothing edifying that can be obtained from a study of history, and for us, that in the realm of history the old materialism is proved to be false, since it fixes active ideal impulses as final causes instead of seeking

FEUERBACH

that which lies behind them, that which is the impulse of these impulses. The lack of logical conclusion does not lie in the fact that ideal impulses are recognized, but in this, that there is no further examination into the more remote causes of their activity. The philosophy of history, on the contrary, particularly as it was treated by Hegel, recognizes that the ostensible and even the real motives of the men who figure in history, are by no means the final causes of historical events, that behind these events stand other moving forces which must be discovered; but it seeks these forces not in history itself, it imports them mostly from the outside, from philosophical ideology, into history. Instead of explaining the history of ancient Greece from its own inner connection, Hegel, for example, explains it solely as if it were nothing but the working out of a beautiful individuality, the realization of art, as such. He says much about the old Greeks that is fine and profound, but this does not prevent our dissatisfaction, now-a-days, with such an explanation, which is mere phraseology.

If, therefore, we set out to discover the

FEUERBACH

impelling forces, which, acknowledged, or unacknowledged, and for the most part unacknowledged, stand behind historical figures, and constitute the true final impulses of history, we cannot consider so much the motives of single individuals, however pre-eminent, as those which set in motion great masses, entire nations, and again, whole classes of people in each nation, and this, too, not in a momentarily flaring and quickly dying flame, but to enduring action culminating in a great historical change. To establish the great impelling forces which play upon the brains of the acting masses and their leaders, the so-called great men, as conscious motives, clear or unclear, directly or ideologically or even in a supernatural form, that is the only method which can place us on the track of the law controlling history as a whole, as well as at particlar periods and in individual lands. All that sets men in motion must act upon their minds, but the force which acts upon the brain depends very largely upon circumstances. The workers have by no means become reconciled to the machine power of the capitalists although they no longer break the

FEUERBACH

machines to pieces as they did on the Rhine in 1848.

But while the discovery of these impelling forces of history was entirely impossible in all other periods, on account of the complicated and hidden interrelations with their effects, our present period has so far simplified these relations that the problem can be solved. Since the establishment of the great industry, at least since the peace of Europe in 1815, it has been no longer a secret to anyone in England that the whole political fight has been for supremacy between two classes, the landed aristocracy and the middle-class. In France, with the return of the Bourbons, the same fact was perceived; the writers of history, from Thierry to Guizot, Mignet, and Thiers in particular, pronounce it as a key to an understanding of French history, especially since the Middle Ages. And since 1830 the working class, the proletariat, has been recognized as the third competitor for mastery in both countries. Circumstances had become so simplified that one would have had to close his eyes not to see in the fight of these three classes and in the conflict of

FEUERBACH

their interests, the moving forces of modern history, at least in the two most advanced countries.

But how came these classes into existence? If the great feudal ancient property in land can have its origin ascribed to political causes through forcible seizure of territories, this could not be done as regards the bourgeoisie and the proletariat. There are in this case clearly exposed the origin and progress of two great economic classes from plain and evident economic causes. And it was just as clear that in the fight between the landholding class and the bourgeoisie, no less than in that between the bourgeoisie and the proletariat, economic interests were the most important, and that political force served only as a mere means of furthering these.

The bourgeoisie and the proletariat both arose as results of a change in economic conditions, or, strictly speaking, in methods of production. The transition, first from hand labor, controlled by the gilds, to manufacture and thence from manufacture to the greater industry, with steam and machine force, has developed these two classes.

FEUERBACH

At a certain stage new forces of production were set in motion by the bourgeoisie, following upon the division of labor and the union of many different kinds of labor in one united manufacture, and the methods of exchange and requirements of exchange developed by their means, were incompatible with the existing historical surviving methods of production consecrated by the law, that is to say the gilds and the innumerable personal and other privileges (which for the unprivileged were only so many fetters) of the feudal social organization. The forces of production brought into being by the bourgeoisie rebelled against the methods of production originated by the gildmasters and the feudal landlords; the result is known; the feudal fetters were struck off, in England gradually, in France at one blow; in Germany the process is not yet quite complete. As manufacture came into conflict at a certain stage of progress with feudal methods of production, so has the greater industry now joined battle with the bourgeois organization of industry established in their place. Bound by this system, owing to the narrow limits of the capi-

FEUERBACH

talistic methods of production, there occurs on the one hand an ever increasing conversion of the mass of the people into proletarians, and on the other hand an ever increasing amount of products which cannot be disposed of. Over-production, and suffering on the part of the masses, the one the cause of the other, that is the absurd contradiction in which it runs its course, and which of necessity requires a control of the forces of production, through a change in the methods of production.

In modern history, at least, it is therefore proved that all political contests are class contests and that all fights of classes for emancipation, in spite of their necessarily political form (for every class struggle is a political struggle), finally, are directed towards economic emancipation. Here, at least, therefore, the State, the political arrangement is the subordinate, bourgeois society, the rule of economic relations, the deciding element. The old fashioned philosophy which even Hegel respected saw in the State the determining element and in bourgeois society the element determined by it. Appearances corresponded with this

FEUERBACH

idea. As all the impulses of each single agent pass through his individual brain and must transform themselves into motives of his will in order to set him to work, so must also the desires of bourgeois society, no matter which class happens to be dominant, penetrate the will of the state in order to secure universal validity in the form of laws. That is the formal side of the matter which is self evident, the question only is what content has this merely formal will—of the individual as well as of the State—and whence comes this content—why is just this desired and nothing else? And if we enquire into this we discover that in modern history the will of the State, as a whole, is declared through the changing needs of bourgeois society, through the domination of this or that class, in the last instance through the development of the forces of production and the conditions of exchange.

But if in our modern times, with their gigantic methods of production and commerce, the State is not an independent affair with an independent development, but its existence as well as its evolution is to be ex-

FEUERBACH

plained in the last resort from the economic conditions of the life of society, so much the more must the same thing be true of all earlier times when the production of the necessities of existence was not furthered by these extensive aids, where, therefore, the necessities of this production must exercise a greater control over men. If the State is today, at the time of the great industries and steam railways, merely, as a whole, the summarized, reflected form of the economic desires of the class which controls production, it must, therefore, have been still more so at a period when a generation of men must spend the greater portion of their united life-time in the satisfaction of their material needs, and man was, therefore, much more dependent on them than we are today. The examination of the earlier epochs of history, as far as it is earnestly conducted in this direction, establishes this abundantly, but manifestly this cannot here be taken in hand.

If the State and public law are the creatures of economic conditions, so, obviously, is private law, which only sanctions relations between individuals under given nor-

FEUERBACH

mal economic circumstances. The form in which this appears may, however, vary considerably. One can, as happened in England in accordance with the whole national development, retain, for the most part, the forms of the old feudal law, and give them a middle-class content, even read a middle-class meaning into the feudal names, but one may also, as in the western part of the European continent, use as a foundation the first general law of a society producing commodities, the Roman, with its unsurpassably keen elaboration, of all the legal relations of possessions of commodities (sellers and buyers, creditors and debtors, contracts, obligations, etc.), by which we can bring it down as common-law to the use and benefit of a still small bourgeois and half feudal society; or, with the help of pseudo-enlightened and moralizing jurists, a code (which is bad from a legal point of view) can be worked out suitable to the conditions of the particular society (as the Prussian land law). And, still again, after a great bourgeois revolution, a classical code for bourgeois society, such as the French "Code Civil," may be worked out. If, therefore,

FEUERBACH

the bourgeois laws only declare the economic circumstances of society, these may be good or bad according to conditions.

In the State appears the first ideological force over men. Society shapes for itself an organ for the protection of its general interests against attack from the outside or inside. This organ is the force of the State. Hardly did it come into being before this organ dominated society, and as a matter of fact, in proportion as it becomes the organ of a particular class, it brings into existence the supremacy of that class. The fight of the subject against the dominant class becomes of necessity political, a fight in the next place against the political control of this latter class. This consciousness of the connection of the political fight with its underlying economic causes becomes more and more obscure and may be altogether lost. Where this is not altogether the case with the combatants it becomes nearly altogether so with the historians. Of the ancient sources of history with regard to the contest within the Roman Republic, Appian alone gives us plain and clear information respecting its final cause, which was prop-

FEUERBACH

erty in land. But the State, once become an independent power over society, forthwith displayed a further ideology. Among the practical politicians and the theorists in jurisprudence, and among the jurists in particular, this fact is first completely lost sight of. Since in each single instance the economic facts must take the form of juristic motives so as to be sanctioned in the form of law, and since, therefore, a backward view must be taken over the whole existing system of law, it follows therefrom that the juristic form appears to be the whole and the economic content nothing at all. Public and private law are considered as independent realms which have their own independent historic evolution, which are considered capable of a systematic representation, and stand in need of it through persistent elimination of all inner contradictions.

Still higher ideological conceptions, i. e., still further removed from the economic foundations, take the form of philosophy and religion. Here, the connection of the ideas with the material conditions of existence become more and more complicated and obscured by reason of the increasing num-

FEUERBACH

ber of links betwen them, but it exists. As the whole Rennaissance from the middle of the fifteenth century was an actual product of the city, and therefore of the bourgeois domination, so was also the philosophy, since that time newly awakened. Its content was actually only the philosophical expression of the thoughts corresponding with the development of the small and middle bourgeois into the great bourgeois. Among the English and French of the preceding century, who were for the most part as good political economists as they were philosophers, this is quite evident, and we have proofs on its very face, as regards the Hegelian school.

Let us now give a slight glance at religion since it appears to stand furthest away from and to be most foreign to material life. Religion arose at a very remote period of human development, in the savage state, from certain erroneous and barbaric conceptions of men with regard to themselves and the outside world of nature around them. Every ideological notion develops, however, when once it has arisen; it grows by additions to the given idea, and develops it fur-

FEUERBACH

ther, otherwise there would be no ideology, that is, no occupation with thoughts as with independent thought-existence, developing independently and subject only to its own laws. That the material conditions of life of the men within whose heads this thought force is at work finally determine the course of this thought-process necessarily remains still unknown to these men, otherwise there would be an entire end of the ideology. These original religious notions, therefore, which are for the most part common to each kindred group of peoples, develop after the separation of the group in a special manner peculiar to each tribe, according to its particular conditions of existence, and this process is for a class of groups of people, and particularly for the Aryans (Indo-Europeans) shown individually by comparative mythology. The gods developed by each tribe were national gods, whose power extended no further than to protect the national territory; beyond the frontier other gods held undisputed sway. They could only be conceived of as existing as long as the nation existed. They fell with its decline. This doctrine

FEUERBACH

of the old nationalities brought about the Roman Empire, whose economic conditions we do not need to examine just now. The old national gods fell, as those of the Romans did also, which were only attached to the narrow limits of the city of Rome. The desire to make the empire a world-empire, by means of a world-wide religion, is clearly shown in the attempts to provide recognition and altars in Rome for all the respectable foreign gods, next to the indigenous ones. But a new world-religion was not to be made in this fashion by imperial decrees. The new world-religion, Christianity, had already arisen in secret by a mixture of combined oriental religions, Jewish theology and popularized Greek philosophy and particularly Stoic philosophy. We must first be at the pains to discover how it originally made its appearance, since its official form as it has come to us is merely that of a State religion, and this end was achieved through the Council of Nice. Enough, the fact that after two hundred and fifty years it was a state religion shows that it was a religion answering to the circumstances of the times. In the Middle Ages it

FEUERBACH

showed itself clearly. In proportion as feudalism developed it grew into a religion corresponding with it, with a hierarchy corresponding to the feudal. And when the rule of the bourgeois came in, it developed into Protestant heresy in antagonism to feudal Catholicism, at first in the South of France, among the Albigenses at the time of the highest growth of the free cities. The Middle Ages had annexed all the surviving forms of ideology, philosophy, politics and jurisprudence, to theology as subordinate parts of theology. It constrained, therefore, all social and political movement to assume a theological form; finally, to the minds of the masses stuffed with religion it was necessary to show their interests in religious guise, in order to raise a tremendous storm. And as the rule of the bourgeois from the beginning brought into being an appendage of propertyless plebeians, with day laborers and servants of all sorts, without any recognized position in their cities, the forerunners of the later proletarians, so the heresy was very early subdivided into a moderate one, on the part of the citizens, and a plebeian revolutionary one, which was an abom-

FEUERBACH

ination to the bourgeois heretics.

The failure to exterminate the protestant heresy corresponded with the invincibility of the rising power of the bourgeois of that time; as this power grew, the fight with the feudal nobles, at first pre-eminently local, began to assume national proportions. The first great conflict occurred in Germany, the so-called Reformation, The power of the bourgeois was neither sufficiently strong nor sufficiently developed for an open rebellious stand, by uniting under the standard of revolt the city plebeians, the smaller nobility, and the peasants of the country districts. The nobility was struck first, the peasants took up a position which was the high-water mark of the entire revolution, the cities left them in the lurch, and so the revolution was left to the leaders of the country gentry who gathered the whole victory to themselves. Thenceforth for three hundred years Germany disappeared from the ranks of independent, energetic progressive countries. But after the German Luther, arose the French Calvin. With natural French acuteness he showed the bourgeois character of the revolution in the Church,

FEUERBACH

republicanised and democratised. While the Lutheran Reformation fell in Germany and Germany declined, the Calvinistic served as a standard to the republicans in Geneva, in Holland, in Scotland, freed Holland from German and Spanish domination, and gave an ideological dress to the second act of the bourgeois revolution which proceeded in England. Here Calvinism proved itself to be the natural religious garb of the interests of the existing rule of the bourgeois and was not realised any further than that the revolution of 1689 was completed by a compromise between a portion of the nobility and the middle-class. The English Established Church was restored, but not in its earlier form with the king for Pope, but was strongly infused with Calvinism. The old-established Church had kept up the merry Catholic Sunday and fought against the tedious Calvinistic one, the new bourgeois Church introduced the latter and added thereby to the charms of England.

In France the Calvinistic minority was subdued in 1685, either made Catholic or hunted out of the country. But what was the good? Directly after that the free think-

FEUERBACH

er Pierre Bayle was at work, and in 1694 Voltaire was born. The tyrannical rule of Louis XIV. only made it easier for the French bourgeoisie to be able to make its revolution in the political form finally suitable to the progressive atheistic bourgeoisie. Instead of Protestants, free-thinkers took their seats in the National Assembly. Thereby Christianity entered upon the last lap of the race. It had become incapable of serving a progressive class any further as the ideological clothing of its efforts, it became more and more the exclusive possession of the dominant classes, and these used it merely as a simple means of government to keep the lower classes in subjection. So then each one of the different classes employed its own suitable religion, the landholding squires catholic jesuitism or protestant orthodoxy, the liberal and radical bourgeois rationalism, and it makes no difference therefore whether people themselves believe in their respective religions or not.

Thus we see religion once arisen contains material of tradition, hence in all ideological matters religion is a great conservative

FEUERBACH

force. But the changes which take place in this material spring from class-conditions, that is from the economic circumstances of the men who take these changes in hand. And that is enough on this part of the subject.

It is only possible at this time to give a general sketch of the Marxian philosophy of history, and particularly as regards illustrations of it. The proof is to be discovered in history itself, and in this regard I may say plainly that it has been sufficiently furnished in other writings. This philosophy, however, makes an end of philosophy in the realm of history, just as the dialectic philosophy of nature renders every philosophy of nature useless or impossible. Practically there is no further need to devise interrelations but to discover them in facts rather. Instead of a philosophy forced from nature and history there remains then only the realm of pure thought—as far as any is left—the teaching of the laws of the thinking process itself, logic and the dialectic.

With the Revolution of 1848 "educated" Germany delivered the challenge to theory

FEUERBACH

and proceeded to action. Hand-labor dependent upon small production and manufacture was done away with by the great industry—Germany again appeared in the world-market. The new particularistic Germany, at all events did away with the most crying anomalies, which the rule of the petty states, the remnants of feudalism and the bureaucratic economy, had placed in the way of their development, but just in proportion as speculation abandoned the studies of philosophers to attain its temple in the Bourse, that great theoretic thought which had been the glory of Germany in the period of its deepest political humiliation, the zeal for pure scientific progress, irrespective of practical, profitable results, and of the disapproval of the police, became lost in educated Germany. It is true that the German official natural science maintained its position, particularly in the field of individual discovery, at the head of its time, but now the American journal "Science" justly remarks that the decisive advances in the matter of the broadest inclusive statement of the relations between single facts, and the harmonising of them

FEUERBACH

with law, are making the greater headway in England, instead of, as earlier, in Germany. And with regard to the sciences of history, philosophy included, with the classical philosophy, the old theoretical spirit, with its carelessness of personal results, first completely disappeared. Thoughtless eclecticism, eager backward glances at a career, and income down to the meanest sycophancy occupy their places. The official representatives of this sort of science have become the open ideologists of the bourgeoisie and the existing state, but at a time when they both stand in open antagonism to the working classes.

Only among the working classes does the German devotion to abstract thought steadily continue to exist. Here it cannot be got rid of. Here we find no backward glances at a career, at profit making, at kindly protection from the upper classes, but on the contrary the more independent and unrestricted the path of science, just so much the more does it find itself in accord with the interests and endeavors of the working class. The new tendency, which in the history of the development of

FEUERBACH

labor made known the key to the understanding of the universal history of society addressed itself in the first place to the working class and found in them the ready acceptance which it neither sought nor expected from official science. The German working-class movement is the heir of the German classical philosphy.

FEUERBACH

APPENDIX.

MARX ON FEUERBACH.

(Jotted down in Brussels in the spring of 1845.)

The chief lack of all materialistic philosophy up to the present, including that of Feuerbach, is that the thing, the reality, sensation is only conceived of under the form of the object which is presented to the eye, but not as human sense—activity, "praxis," not subjectively. It therefore came about that the active side in opposition to materialism was developed from idealism, but only abstractly; this was natural, since idealism does not recognize real tangible facts as such. Feuerbach is willing, it is true, to distinguish objects of sensation from objects existing in thought, but he conceives of human activity itself not as objective activity. He, therefore, in the "Wesen des Christenthums," regards only theoretical activity as generally human, while the "praxis" is conceived and fixed only in its disgusting form.

FEUERBACH

II.

The question if objective truth is possible to human thought is not a theoretical but a practical question. In practice man must prove the truth, that is the reality and force in his actual thoughts. The dispute as to the reality or non-reality of thought which separates itself, "the praxis," is a purely scholastic question.

III.

The materialistic doctrine that men are the products of conditions and education, different men therefore the products of other conditions and changed education, forgets that circumstances may be altered by men and that the educator has himself to be educated. It necessarily happens therefore that society is divided into two parts, of which one is elevated above society (Robert Owen for example).

The occurrence simultaneously of a change in conditions and human activity can only be comprehended and rationally understood as a revolutionary fact.

FEUERBACH

IV.

Feuerbach proceeds from a religious self-alienation, the duplication of the world into a religious, imaginary, and a real world. His work consists in the discovery of the material foundations of the religious world. He overlooked the fact that after carrying this to completion the important matter still remains unaccomplished. The fact that the material foundation annuls itself and establishes for itself a realm in the clouds can only be explained from the heterogeneity and self-contradiction of the material foundation. This itself must first become understood in its contradictions and so become thoroughly revolutionized by the elimination of the contradiction. After the earthly family has been discovered as the secret of the Holy Family, one must have theoretically criticised and theoretically revolutionised it beforehand.

V.

Feuerbach, not satisfied with abstract thought, invokes impressions produced by the senses, but does not comprehend sensation as practical sensory activities.

FEUERBACH

VI.

Feuerbach dissolves religion in humanity. But humanity is not an abstraction dwelling in each individual. In its reality it is the ensemble of the conditions of society.

Feuerbach, who does not enquire into this fact, is therefore compelled:

1. To abstract religious sentiment from the course of history, to place it by itself, and to pre-suppose an abstract, isolated, human individual.

2. Humanity is therefore only comprehended by him as a species, as a hidden sort of merely natural identity of qualities in which many individuals are embraced.

VII.

Therefore Feuerbach does not see that religious feeling is itself a product of society, and that the abstract individual which he analyses belongs in reality to a certain form of society.

The life of society is essentially practical. All the mysteries which seduce speculative thought into mysticism find their solution in

FEUERBACH

human practice and in concepts of this practice.

IX.

The highest point to which materialism attains, that is the materialism which comprehends sensation, not as a practical fact, is the point of view of the single individual in bourgeois society.

X.

The standpoint of the old materialism is "bourgeois" society; the standpoint of the new, human society, or associated humanity.

XI.

Philosophers have only interpreted the world differently, but the point is to change it.